About the Author:

A graduate of Biola College, Talbot Theological Seminary, Western Baptist Seminary and Grace Theological Seminary, CURTIS C. MITCHELL, Th.D., is convinced that prayer is crucial in accomplishing God's work in the world. A popular speaker at Bible conferences, youth retreats and student assemblies, he has traveled throughout Europe and the Middle East and has served as Bible Lands lecturer for Biola College.

Praying Jesus' Way

By Curtis C. Mitchell

LET'S LIVE!
PRAYING JESUS' WAY

Praying 'Jesus' Way

A new approach to personal prayer

Curtis C. Mitchell

Fleming H. Revell Company
Old Tappan, New Jersey

Unless otherwise identified, Scripture quotations are from the King James Version of the Bible.

Scripture quotations identified RSV are from the Revised Standard Version of the Bible, copyrighted 1946, 1952, © 1971 and 1973.

Library of Congress Cataloging in Publication Data

Mitchell, Curtis C., 1927, date
    Praying Jesus' way.

    1. Jesus Christ—Prayers. 2. Prayer.
I. Title.
BV229.M57   248'.3   76–49879
ISBN 0–8007–0843–1

TO my prayer partners at Biola College:
Dr. Clyde Cook, Col. Burton Hatch,
Dr. Lloyd Kwast, and Rev. Ernie Peirson.
Our weekly prayer sessions
have confirmed the biblical principles
set forth in this volume.

Contents

Foreword by Joyce Landorf   9
Introduction   11

Part One
The Prayer Habits of Jesus   **15**

1 Prayer Habits During Christ's First Two Years   17
2 Prayer Habits During the First Part of Christ's Final Year of Ministry   21
3 Prayer Habits During the Last Part of Jesus' Final Year of Ministry   25
4 Instances From Passion Week to Ascension   30
5 Concluding Thoughts on Christ's Prayer Habits   36

Part Two
The Major Prayers of Jesus   **39**

6 The Lord's Prayer   41
7 The High Priestly Prayer   49
8 The Prayer in Gethsemane   59
9 The Prayers From the Cross   68

Part Three
The Prayer Teachings of Jesus   **75**

10 Teachings Concerning Prayer Attitudes   77
11 Teachings Concerning Persistence   83
12 Teachings Concerning Content   89
13 Teachings Concerning Prayer Conditions (Part One)   95
14 Teachings Concerning Prayer Conditions (Part Two)   104

Part Four
The Prayer Principles of Jesus **115**

15 The Significance, Nature, and Content of Prayer 117
16 Prayer Attitudes and Procedures 134
17 Prayer Conditions and Concluding Remarks 145

Foreword

I had finished singing the solo for the service at Hume Lake chapel so I settled down to listen to the speaker of the evening, Dr. Curtis C. Mitchell.

As soon as he introduced his subject on prayer I mentally reached up, took my superspiritual cape off a peg, and smugly wrapped myself inside to nap a bit. After all, I had read every book on prayer, I had had a great praying mother, and I had experienced firsthand all there was to know about prayer—or so I thought.

Within five minutes my thick spiritual cape of smugness had melted off my shoulders exactly as if it had been made of Jello and had just been hit by a hot blowtorch.

I was utterly astounded by my alarming lack of knowledge about Jesus' personal prayer life or His direct teachings on prayer. There I sat, a child of God, a Jesus person, yet totally ignorant of Jesus' attitudes or procedures involving prayer!

Doctor Mitchell's sermon began in me a challenge and a wish that night. I began to search out the Scriptures I had heard and I wished that Doctor Mitchell would write a book on prayer for all of us.

In the brief years since that night at Hume Lake I've seen both the challenge and the wish come into existence. How good God is!

You may find that this book shatters some of your pet concepts or cherished prayer formulas, but don't let that stop you from reading it. The author gives us ample authority from Jesus' teachings which validates his positions on prayer.

There is much to be learned from this enlightening, informative book and, once read, it should then be studied.

Remember the disciples *never* asked Jesus to teach them *anything* —except how to pray. It was as vital then as now to our Christian union with God and others—and we must be found *Praying Jesus' Way!*

JOYCE LANDORF

Introduction

Have you ever stopped to think about the fact that God does not usually do things the way we do? Would you have captured the city of Jericho by having your men walk around it blowing horns? Would you have thought to remind Gideon to stock up on water jars before his battle with the Midianites? Would you have chosen some other seagoing vessel for Jonah's voyage to Nineveh? The fact is that we are clearly told that God's ways are not our ways (*see* Isaiah 59:8,9).

One of the great problems in living our Christian lives is that we often insist upon doing things our way rather than God's way. We don't need new methods, we need desperately to get back to the old methods—the biblical way of doing things.

Shortly before He went to the cross, Jesus gathered His eleven key men around Him for a final briefing session. These eleven men would be responsible (humanly speaking) for carrying out Christ's program on earth after His ascension. In this final, crucial meeting (*see* John 14–17), Jesus reiterated six times, "If you ask . . . I will do" (*see* John 14:13). When Jesus Christ repeats something six times in one meeting, you and I had better sit up and take notice. I submit to you that Jesus was giving His disciples a formula for action. He was telling them how to really accomplish things in divine style.

In this simple statement, prayer is set forth as the *primary human factor in the accomplishment of God's program on earth.* With a startling boldness, Christ asserted that divine action, in some mysterious manner, is conditioned upon believing prayer. Thus prayer is set forth as the chief task of the believer. It is *his* responsibility to ask. It is God's responsibility to accomplish. This twofold division of responsibility (our asking and God's doing) can be seen in the early church. A close study of the Book of Acts will reveal that the believers fervently and persistently asked and God responded. In light of this, it is difficult to envision the successful functioning of God's program,

11

be it individual or corporate, apart from the consistent and proper ministry of prayer. In fact, it appears that failure in prayer will mean failure in the effective functioning of the individual (or the group) so far as God's work is concerned.

I have personally discovered that prayer, as taught in the New Testament, is not always the same as prayer taught in current books about the subject. When I began studying the Bible and its teachings on prayer, many of my former concepts had to be completely changed or revised.

Today the subject of prayer has been relegated to the realm of the devotional. Its treatment is usually rather light and fluffy. Somewhere along the line, prayer has been divorced from solid New Testament doctrine. This book will be an attempt to correct this trend. Therefore, my aim is to set forth solid biblical evidence by examining every teaching and every allusion to prayer Jesus made in the Gospels.

Acknowledgments

My appreciation to Rev. Ernie Peirson for his constructive sugges-
tions and encouragement while reading the manuscript, and to Mr.
Dave Briggs for his extensive, yet excellent, editorial work on this
volume.

PART ONE
THE PRAYER HABITS OF JESUS

Beyond doubt the greatest examples of correct prayer practice ever displayed were those demonstrated by Jesus Christ. So distinct was His prayer life that by simply observing it our Lord's disciples were motivated to request instruction on the subject (*see* Luke 11:1).

And since my purpose is to edify the saints, not "snow the saints," I suggest that this volume be read with the Bible at your elbow for maximum benefit.

We can see that Christ intended His prayer to be an example for His disciples from the several instances when He seems to have deliberately engaged in private prayer within their sight. On at least one occasion He intentionally took His three key men on a prayer excursion (*see* Luke 9:28), and the text makes it plain that only Christ prayed. The obvious implication is that He took them with Him as observers. Thus the *example* of Christ was to be the *practice* of His followers.

1
Prayer Habits During Christ's First Two Years

The Gospel writers record four distinct incidents when Jesus engaged in prayer during the first two years of His public ministry.

Prayer at His Baptism: Luke 3:21–23. All of the Gospel writers record the baptism of Christ, but only Luke mentions the fact that during the baptismal ritual He was actually engaged in prayer. Note if you will the actual words of Luke 3:21: ". . . Jesus also being baptized, and praying, the heaven was opened. . . ." The grammar indicates a continuous activity in prayer which was interrupted by the dramatic opening of the heavens and the booming voice of the Father.

Some Bible teachers are of the opinion that the opening of the heavens was in fact the Father's answer to the prayers of Jesus. While this cannot be affirmed with absolute certainty, I personally am inclined to agree. At any rate, it can be said with certainty that while Jesus was engaged in prayer, God in a miraculous manner confirmed His earthly mission as the official Messiah.

There are several truths concerning prayer that we may learn from this simple incident. The fact that Jesus prayed on that very special occasion indicates something of the prominence of prayer in His life. In this instance prayer is envisioned as a precise, overt act, not simply a vague attitude of personal communion with the Father. Furthermore, there is a distinct possibility that in this case, prayer was effective in actually causing the heavens to open! Wow! What a graphic example of the effectiveness of prayer. Prayer produced results—positive, powerful results!

Prayer During Christ's First Preaching Tour: Mark 1:35. Christ is now in the first flush of His popularity. The preceding day had been packed with activity for our Lord. Beyond question it had been a long, exhausting day, yet we read that, "In the morning, rising up a great while before day, he went out, and departed into a solitary place, and there prayed" (*see* Mark 1:35). The expressions "rising up" and "went out" grammatically indicate a decisive action, not simply an attitude. Our Lord is said to have gone into "the desert, early in the morning when still dark." In all probability this was to avoid people and other distractions. Thus both the *time* and the *place* seem to indicate a deliberate attempt on the part of Christ to get alone and pray. Christ was still engaged in prayer when the disciples found Him. The conversation that took place gives us a hint as to the purpose which prompted Jesus to pray.

Jesus' popularity was due largely to His healing ministry, but after this prayer session He announced to His disciples that He had decided to move on and preach. (*See* Mark 1:37,38.)

To be sure, healing had its place as a means of authenticating His Person and message. However, it was not intended to become an end in itself, which was exactly what the people apparently desired. So Jesus' prayer burden on this occasion seemed to be, "Is all of this popularity caused by healing really consistent with My mission?" For this He sought guidance.

Several factors can be inferred from this incident. Certainly it points out our Lord's preference for solitude during serious prayer sessions. Otherwise, why didn't He just pray in the house after breakfast? The absence of any significant or unusual event in the context may well serve to indicate that prayer sessions were somewhat normal to our Lord's daily routine. To be sure, Jesus wasn't simply a "foxhole" prayer warrior. We also learn that prayer was a deliberate, volitional act. In all probability it was a prayer session of some length, because a man would hardly arise at such an inconvenient hour to trudge out into the desert for a few moments of prayer.

Finally, it must once again be stated that prayer for Jesus was of *primary* significance. Therefore, if prayer was of such importance to Christ as a man, of how much greater importance should it be for you and me?

Second Incident on the First Healing Tour: Luke 5:16. Not long after the incident just described, we find our Lord again resorting to prayer. He had healed a leper who disregarded His express command and began to publish widely the fact of his remarkable healing. This

quite naturally attracted even greater crowds (*see* Luke 5:15). In the
face of this exploding popularity, Jesus ". . . withdrew himself into the
wilderness, and prayed" (Luke 5:16).

The word *withdrew* grammatically describes a *habitual action*
rather than a *single act*. The picture portrayed is quite vivid. The
crowds, wild with enthusiasm over Christ's healing powers, were
continuously gathering around Him day after day (*see* verse 15), while
Jesus, at every opportunity, would slip quietly away from these
throngs and pray.

Jesus would often slip away from the multitudes to seek guidance
from the Father. Very likely, He would say, "Father, My human ego
is really gratified by all of the fame I'm receiving, but I'm not on this
earth to simply make a big name for Myself. I'm on this earth to do
Your will. Father, what should I do? Should I stay and bask in the
popularity, or should I move on and deliver Your message to Israel?"

The text makes it plain that these distinct times of prayer were not
carried on in accordance with some prearranged prayer schedule. The
implications are that Christ felt such a need to pray that at every
possible opportunity He would break away for a time with the Father.

Note, too, that in the very nature of the case, Christ's prayers on
these occasions would be petitionary in nature. By that I mean Christ
would ask the Father for something for which He felt a desperate
need. Let's face it, a man doesn't break away from a mob to seek an
audience with God just to engage in small talk!

The Choice of the Twelve: Luke 6:12. The exact time of this event
is not known for sure. Most scholars place the event shortly before
Christ delivered the Sermon on the Mount. If this is the case, then our
Lord had been undergoing a period of both opposition and fame. The
Pharisees had accused His disciples of violating tradition by plucking
wheat on the Sabbath. Furthermore, they were "filled with madness"
because Jesus had healed a man on the Sabbath (Luke 6:11). They had
actually joined forces with the Herodians in trying to figure out a way
to destroy Him. Yet with the common people, Christ's popularity
remained at a high level. Great crowds continued to press Him for
healing. It was "in those days, that he went out into a mountain to
pray, and continued all night in prayer to God" (Luke 6:12).

The language clearly indicates that the only reason our Lord took the trouble to climb that mountain was to pray. He wasn't simply out for some exercise, and after hiking around for a while decided it might be nice to pray. His prayer session on that occasion lasted "all night." The word translated "all night" is a medical term and was used in Greek literature to describe the all-night vigil of a doctor as he waited intently at the bedside of a patient. The very word conveys the picture of urgency, earnestness, and intensity.

Though the passage does not state in so many words the purpose for this deliberate, all-night prayer vigil, all commentators unite in recognizing that it was in some manner associated with the decision expressed in the next verse: "And when it was day, he called unto him his disciples: and of them he chose twelve, whom also he named apostles" (Luke 6:13). There can be little doubt of the fact that the human Jesus sought illumination and guidance concerning the momentous decision He was about to make. Of all His disciples, whom should He select for positions of special leadership? Humanly speaking, the right choice was necessary for the success of His program. So prior to making the decision Christ earnestly sought guidance from the Father.

Perhaps the two most impressive aspects of this incident are its lengthy duration and the intense nature of the praying. Most probably His praying was in the nature of petitions wherein our Lord sought guidance in His forthcoming decision.

As the night wore on and He received direction as to which men should be selected, His prayer perhaps shifted to intercession. He began to ask the Father to strengthen and enrich the men He now knew He would select. Intercession is asking God on behalf of others. It is a specialized form of petition. Though we may not understand completely *why* and *how* prayer works, it cannot be denied that Jesus believed in and practiced prayer *seriously!*

2
Prayer Habits During the First Part of Christ's Final Year of Ministry

While the Gospel writers recorded only four prayer incidents during the first two years of our Lord's public ministry, in the first six months of His final year on earth, five distinct incidents are recorded.

Before the Feeding of the Five Thousand: Matthew 14:19; Mark 6:41; Luke 9:16; John 6:11. Jesus made it His consistent practice to thank the Father before partaking of food. The first recorded instance of this is in the account of the feeding of the five thousand. All four Gospel writers make note of the fact that Christ prayed upon this occasion.

The expression "He blessed" (*see* Matthew 14:19) refers to the blessing of an object or simply praise to God. Therefore, Christ's prayer on this occasion was not in the nature of a petition (asking God for something), but rather thanksgiving offered to the Father for His provisions. No real connection between the prayer and the miracle can be established. He is not asking God to do something but is praising and thanking Him. This gives unquestioned verification for the Christian practice of giving thanks to God for daily food.

After the Feeding of the Five Thousand: Matthew 14:23; Mark 6:46; John 6:14,15. After the five thousand had eaten, Jesus promptly dismissed the crowd, ordered His disciples to cross the lake ahead of Him, and He "went up into a mountain apart to pray . . ." (Matthew 14:23). The grammar makes it plain that Christ's action in dispersing the crowd was deliberate and personal. The obvious reason for Christ's unusual behavior is clearly revealed in John's account: "When Jesus therefore preceived that they would come and take him by force, to make him a king, he departed again into a mountain himself alone" (John 6:15). A new crisis had been reached, hence Jesus must pray. What a tremendous temptation it must have been for the human Jesus. Here was an opportunity to be king apart from suffering, apart from the cross. How easy it would have been for Him to rationalize at this time. He needed counsel to reassure Him of the right course of action, and He needed strength to follow that course.

This incident is rich in instruction. Perhaps most obvious are the frantic, *deliberate* efforts Christ made personally. It necessitated the expulsion of both the mob and His disciples, as well as a climb into the mountains. Prayer was obviously not a plaything. It was a necessity.

It becomes evident once more that His praying in this instance must have been largely *petitionary* in nature. This is not to disavow the conversational aspect in Christ's prayer life. To be sure, it was no doubt present in this instance, but *petition* (asking) was the primary factor in this specific prayer session.

At the Feeding of the Four Thousand: Matthew 15:36; Mark 8:6,7. Mark indicates that Jesus prayed two times: for the bread and for the fish: "And he commanded the people to sit down on the ground: and he took the seven loaves, and gave thanks . . . . And they had a few small fishes: and he blessed, and commanded to set them also before them" (Mark 8:6,7).

Those familiar with the cultural situation contend that the double blessing was necessary because the people were Gentiles rather than Jews. When feeding the five thousand earlier, Jesus gave thanks only once in strict accordance with Jewish custom. If He had given the blessing but once before these Gentiles, they would have thought that it was only for the bread. Hence, to avoid any misconception, Jesus prayed over both the bread and the fish.

From all of this we again learn that Jesus consistently blessed food before partaking, and that His praying included thanksgiving. More significantly, this incident points up the fact that the offering of public prayers is at times at least designed to affect the hearers as well as God. Otherwise why did Jesus comply with Gentile custom by offering a dual prayer?

Before the Confession of Peter: Luke 9:18. Jesus is now well into the last year of His ministry. The opposition of the Jewish leaders has greatly increased in intensity. His popularity among the ordinary people is still quite strong, though beginning to wane. The inability of the crowds to understand some of His concepts becomes ever more apparent. Many followers have already left Him. At the time of this prayer, Jesus had withdrawn for the fourth time to get alone with His disciples and instruct them.

Another crisis had arisen in our Lord's ministry. Amid all of the misunderstanding which prevailed about Him, would His disciples also misunderstand? Prior to asking His disciples the crucial question "Whom say ye that I am?" (Luke 9:20) Jesus engaged in a session of prayer that preceded a momentous incident.

In this situation, Jesus once again ". . . was alone praying . . ." (Luke 9:18). Yet, strangely the text continues by saying that " . . . his disciples were with him. . . ." How could this be? Probably the phrase "was alone" should be taken to mean "in private" or "in a solitary spot" apart from the multitudes, but *in the presence of His disciples.* The word translated "praying" indicates that only Jesus was praying.

We can learn several things from this incident. Once more Christ is seen praying in a time of crisis. The fact that His disciples were allowed to be present would seem to indicate that in some manner His praying was intended to have an effect upon them. Perhaps the sight of their Master praying would stimulate in them a desire for prayer.

Finally, the fact that this prayer was evidently related to His subsequent questioning of the disciples would seem to indicate that it must have been petitionary in nature. Note if you will that following Peter's confession, Christ acknowledged it had been supernaturally given! Could it be that Christ had been asking the Father to give the disciples enlightenment? Again, prayer produced results! Christ's way of accomplishment was through prayer!

Before the Transfiguration: Luke 9:28, 29. Matthew, Mark, and Luke all record the transfiguration, but only Luke makes note of the fact that Jesus was praying at the time. Jesus took three disciples "and went up into a mountain to pray" (Luke 9:28). The grammar makes it crystal clear that the avowed purpose of the excursion was for prayer and that again only Jesus actually prayed.

Evidently His prayer session was quite lengthy because the transformation occurred while He was praying, and verse 32 reveals that when the miracle actually took place, the disciples "were heavy with sleep." Thus while Christ was praying, the disciples fell asleep and were awakened by the miracle.

The fact that once again the audible voice of the Father was heard (*see* Luke 9:35) is of interest. As noted earlier in discussing His baptism, each time the Father's voice was heard Christ was engaged in active prayer. It is possible, then, that prayer prompted the miracle. This possibility is heightened when we compare the accounts of Matthew and Mark of the incident. Matthew and Mark give the distinct impression that Jesus went into the mountain *to be transfigured!* Yet Luke clearly says it was *to pray!* Christ evidently had two purposes in mind as He set out with the three disciples that morning—to pray and to be transfigured.

For the second time Christ is seen *deliberately* engaged in private prayer *in the presence of His disciples.* Could this imply that prayer can have certain legitimate psychological effects upon persons who simply observe the process? Does this suggest that it might be wise for parents to allow their children to see them engaged in prayer? Indeed, my wife can personally testify to the profound effect of inadvertently coming upon one of her parents praying. One such experience was of greater value than many formal Sunday-school lessons on prayer—I can assure you.

3
Prayer Habits During the Last Part of Jesus' Final Year of Ministry

Up to this point, the prayer instances in the life of Christ have contained nothing of the specific content of His prayers. From this point on, almost all references will include the words He said while praying.

At the Return of the Seventy: Matthew 4:25 and Luke 10:21. After rebuking certain cities because of unbelief, Christ "rejoiced in spirit, and said, I thank thee, O Father, Lord of heaven and earth, that thou hast hid these things from the wise and prudent, and hast revealed them unto babes: even so, Father; for so it seemed good in thy sight" (Luke 10:21). In this act of prayer Jesus is said to have "rejoiced in spirit." This is clearly a reference to the Holy Spirit and not Jesus' human spirit, as a study of virtually all modern translations will bear out. The joyous prayer uttered by Jesus is verbalized by the sentence "I thank thee" (Luke 10:21), which carries the idea of continual open praise. An expanded translation might well read, "I continuously and openly confess and exalt Thee."

Notice that Jesus made no direct formal preparation for this prayer as He had done on many previous occasions. He didn't send His disciples away or climb a mountain! He simply burst forth in praise! Evidently the joyous report of His disciples (*see* Luke 10:17) triggered a spontaneous and highly emotional response in Christ. It is important to note that Jesus' humanity comes very much into focus in His prayer life. Actually Christ only needed to pray because He was human. Deity never needs to pray. It was because He chose to impose limits upon Himself and function as a dependent human being that He needed to pray! Only a *dependent* person prays!

The content of Christ's praise seems to center in the fact that the Father, as Sovereign ("Lord of heaven and earth"), had "hid" certain things from one type of people, and "revealed" these same things to another type of people. (*See* Luke 10:21.) Thus Christ's praise was motivated by God's *great, sovereign, providential acts.* Our Lord was praising the Father for the fact that He is in control and running the show! In this crazy world that's really a comforting thought. No doubt all of us should praise God for the fact that He has a plan and it's being worked out no matter how confusing the situation appears to us down here on planet earth.

This is obviously not a lengthy prayer but it is really loaded with insights. For openers, did you notice that for the first time the ministry of the Holy Spirit is associated with prayer? Christ prayed in the Spirit! Evidently the Holy Spirit prompted the jubilant outburst. Clearly it is Jesus praying in audible, understandable language, but doing so under the controlling influence of the Spirit. I point this out because I have been told by some of my fellow believers that praying in the Spirit involves praying in an unknown tongue! But it seems safe to say that a person can pray in the Spirit without praying in tongues. The two expressions "praying in the Spirit" and "praying in tongues" are not necessarily synonymous terms!

Certainly this incident brings out *emotional* involvement in prayer. Obviously this was no emotionless, monotonous, ritual type of prayer. There is also no hint of any formal preparation. He assumed no particular position, nor did He face in a certain direction. He did not even seek to be alone. He just burst forth in praise. Yet, in spite of its evident emotion and spontaneity, the prayer was completely reverent as seen by the use of the closing reverential form of the words translated "in thy sight."

Before leaving this incident let me make two more observations. Christ shockingly addressed Jehovah-God by the title "Father." In fact, the prayer begins and ends with the title. This was probably one of the most revolutionary aspects of Jesus' prayer.

The Jews held Jehovah in such awe that they would not even pronounce that name. Yet Jesus came along and addressed Him in a very intimate filial (child-parent) manner. Note also, if you will, that Christ was very *specific* in designating the precise reasons for His praise. He didn't just say, "Father, thank You for Your sovereignty," or "Father, I praise You because You control history." No, He pinpointed exactly the details of God's dealings for which He was grateful. So often we are guilty of vague, generalized, almost ambiguous praying. Jesus was not!

Prior to Giving the Lord's Prayer: Luke 11:1. Jesus is now only months away from the cross. His disciples have been His constant companions for well over two years. They had listened to Him deliver the famous Sermon on the Mount wherein He had given considerable teaching on prayer. Yet the record states that on one occasion "as he was praying in a certain place, when he ceased, one of his disciples said unto him, Lord, teach us to pray, as John also taught his disciples" (Luke 11:1).

Though the disciples were in close proximity, the language again indicates that Christ alone was engaged in prayer. Again, the word translated "praying" cannot possibly be construed as a prayerful attitude or a direction of the soul Godward. The praying was going on in a specific locale ("in a certain place"), and it had a precise time of termination ("when he ceased").

The language strongly suggests that it was the sight of their praying Master that prompted the disciples to make the request "Lord, teach us to pray." The request is further defined: " . . . as John also taught his disciples." This indicates that John the Baptist probably advanced the concepts of prayer beyond the teachings of traditional Judaism.

Several truths may be implied from this unique request of the disciples. It suggests that Jesus' praying was distinct from contemporary Jewish practice. Their request indicates that they considered prayer the key to spiritual success in the Man they had lived with, in the closest possible association, for more than two and a half years.

At the Grave of Lazarus: John 11:41, 42. In this dramatic setting, " . . . Jesus lifted up his eyes, and said, Father, I thank thee that thou hast heard me. And I knew that thou hearest me always: but because of the people which stand by I said it, that they may believe that thou hast sent me" (John 11:41, 42).

Evidently two distinct prayers of our Lord are in view in John 11:41. Christ gives thanks specifically for a previous prayer concerning Lazarus. This prayer had probably been uttered when Christ *first* heard the news concerning His friend. I say this because at the time that Jesus heard the news, He told His disciples that Lazarus was indeed dead and that He would awaken him (*see* John 11:11). The reason Christ could assure His disciples that He would awaken Lazarus was that He had already prayed for his resurrection! He knew that His prayers were always answered (*see* John 11:42). In essence, then, the prayer recorded in these verses was an expression of joyous assurance and thanksgiving for *answered* prayer.

The content of Christ's thanksgiving is really a general statement concerning all of Christ's prayers. Christ knew with absolute certainty that the Father heeded all of His prayers. Each time Christ prayed He was certain of being heard.

The question has been raised as to why the Lord uttered this prayer of thanksgiving publicly. The obvious answer, as stated by Christ, was, " . . . I said it, that they may believe that thou hast sent me" (John 14:42). His prayer was a testimony to the people that the miracle they were about to witness was performed by the power of God in *direct answer to prayer!* It is becoming obvious that prayer was the means utilized by the human Jesus to get things done!

From this rather dramatic incident we can learn a great deal. Once again, in a crisis, Christ typically resorted to prayer as His *first* recourse. The initial prayer which eventually resulted in the miracle would have to have been intercessory in nature. Remember that intercession is asking God to do something for someone else. This intercession on behalf of others was heard by the Father and produced dramatic results.

The prayer of thanksgiving uttered beside the grave of Lazarus closely followed Christ's general pattern. But I would have you make note of how very specific Christ was as to *what* He was thankful for and *why* He was thankful. As noted earlier, Christ never prayed in generalities either in petition or thanksgiving.

Of greater significance is the rather startling statement that Christ's prayers were always heard and answered. In fact, Christ was so confident that His prayer for Lazarus's resurrection had been answered that He actually thanked the Father publicly *prior* to the miracle! The basic reason for such confidence was the fact that Christ was always in complete conformity to the will of the Father. His meat and drink was to do the Father's will, so all of His prayers were in accordance with the Father's will and certain of being answered.

Finally, it should be noted that *public* prayer, (just like Christ's private prayer in front of His disciples) can be legitimately used to affect the hearers. I have often been told that when a person prays publicly, he should try to be oblivious to the audience and address his prayers as if only God would hear. It was said that public prayer, like private prayer, should be addressed only to the Father "which seeth in secret" (Matthew 6:4). Yet the wording of this prayer was obviously intended for the audience as well as the Father! Public prayer can legitimately be used as an educational tool!

During family devotions I can remember my parents cleverly phrasing their prayers in such a manner that while talking to God they delivered a message to me! After I had whaled the daylights out of my younger brother they would subtly ask God to help us all learn to be kind and considerate of each other. As a child I got the message, and couched in a solemn prayer to God it had a greater wallop than a direct exhortation to me!

At the Blessing of Children: Matthew 19:13. It was customary for Jewish mothers to bring their children to an honorable person that He might bless them. Luke, in his account of the incident (*see* Luke 18:15), uses the word *infants,* which indicates very young children probably incapable of understanding what Jesus was doing to them.

Mark records that He took the infants into His arms and "blessed them" (Mark 10:16). The word Mark uses is actually a compound word. It is the usual word for "bless" but with a preposition attached to it that adds the concept of *intensity,* the idea being that Christ did not bless them in a simple, matter-of-fact manner, but with fervor and *intensity!* To me this is a graphic example that for Jesus prayer *always* included emotional involvement. If ever there should have been a time when Jesus might have been expected to offer up an emotionally detached ritual prayer, this would have been the time. Yet clearly He prayed with real earnestness.

Because this prayer-blessing was given in public it probably implies that there were certain psychological values intended—in this instance psychological benefits to the parents because the children were too young to understand.

4

Instances From Passion Week to Ascension

Beyond question the final week of our Lord's ministry prior to His Crucifixion was the most intense of His entire earthly sojourn. All Gospel writers give great emphasis to it. Passion Week was also a time heightened by prayer activity. Four distinct instances are recorded during that one week alone.

At the Coming of Certain Greeks: John 12:27, 28. Upon viewing the Greeks, Jesus immediately began to speak of His "hour," an evident reference to the cross and all its implications. As He proceeded to speak of His coming death, His emotional involvement seemed to rapidly intensify. In this emotionally troubled state Jesus uttered a prayer: " . . . Father, save me from this hour: but for this cause came I unto this hour. Father, glorify thy name" (John 12:27, 28).

This prayer cannot possibly be understood apart from its emotional context. This setting is brought sharply into focus by the phrase "Now is my soul troubled . . ." (John 12:27). The troubled area is stipulated as His soul. In this emotional center Jesus is said to be "troubled". The word is very strong and means to be deeply stirred and agitated.

Thus this prayer seems to be a spontaneous, verbal manifestation of profound emotions that had been building up within the soul of Jesus. I'm sure we've all had emotions build up within us over a period of time, and then suddenly burst forth. That seems to be the picture here.

The King James Version makes the sentence "Father, save me from this hour" an actual prayer request on the part of Jesus. However, most commentators object to this. They feel that if Christ actually prayed this, He would have been desiring something contrary to the Father's will. So, many commentators and translators take these words as a simple question rather than a prayer request. According to this view, Jesus, in a highly disturbed state, was simply saying,

"Should I say, Father, save Me from this hour? No! That wouldn't be right because that's the very reason I came into the world in the first place!" This seems to me to be the correct understanding of Christ's statement.

The actual prayer probably consisted of the simple request "Father, glorify thy name." The basic idea in the word translated "glorify" is *to shine forth* or *show forth* in a favorable manner. In this case the object to be glorified was the Father's name. In Jewish thinking, "name" meant almost the same thing as "person" or "character." Therefore, Christ, in spite of obvious emotional distress due to His forthcoming appointment at Calvary, was obviously concerned that ultimately God's character might stand out before men in all its power, grace, truth, love, and majesty. Eventually the Father did just that, for the death, burial, and Resurrection of Christ displayed more of the glorious qualities of God than any other single event in history. The words of this request are few, but the sense is immense.

It is worthwhile to note that at the completion of this prayer there came "a voice from heaven . . ." (John 12:28). That the voice was audible there can be no doubt because of the reaction of the people (*see* John 12:29). They could not make out the words, but all knew that they had heard something. Interestingly, this is the third and final time the voice of the Father was heard, and as noted, each time it was in connection with prayer.

The intense emotional context of the prayer is worthy of special notice. Christ was always emotional in His praying to some degree at least, but in this instance it was extremely intense. Also, Christ's emotions are pinpointed as arising out of His humanity (His *soul* was troubled). Prayer sprang from emotional need! No sane person could read this incident and view it simply as a pious example for Jesus' followers to emulate! Prayer was a very *real* and *necessary* thing to Christ!

Clearly the prayer was in the nature of a petition. This is somewhat unique in that up to this point Christ's *public* prayers had always been in the nature of thanksgiving or praise. It seems that basically in private He petitioned—in public He praised!

In this instance no formal preparations were made for prayer. It seems rather to be in the nature of an unpremeditated emotional outburst. Perhaps such outbursts were often uttered in the solitude of the desert or mountain.

Finally, let us take note of the fact that this prayer expresses the ultimate motive for biblical prayer: the glory of God. Did Jesus' request glorify God? Was it in harmony with Divine will? Yes! These are primary conditions for successful New Testament praying.

At the Lord's Supper: Matthew 26:26,27; Mark 14:22, 23; Luke 22:17–19. The setting is familiar. Christ and His disciples are gathered in a borrowed room for a final meal together, on the eve of His trial. Toward the close of the meal, "Jesus took bread, and blessed it. . . . And he took the cup, and gave thanks . . ." (Matthew 26:26, 27). The grammar indicates that the prayer was not the significant factor in the scene. Prayer was simply mentioned in connection with the institution of the Communion service. Probably the most unusual aspect to the entire incident was the *time* at which our Lord uttered these words of praise. It was just before Gethsemane—just before Calvary! Certainly this has to be a vivid example of Paul's later admonition "In every thing give thanks" (1 Thessalonians 5:18).

Prayer for Peter: Luke 22:32. We are now in the shadow of the cross. In this setting Jesus specifically addresses Peter and informs him that "Satan hath desired to have you, that he may sift you as wheat: But I have prayed for thee, that thy faith fail not . . ." (Luke 22:31, 32). This announcement to Peter was not actually a prayer, but it does indicate the nature and content of a *prior* prayer.

Christ informed Peter that Satan desired him. Actually the original text reads, "*the* Satan." This is probably an attempt by Christ to allude to the incident in the first chapter of Job: "Peter, the same devil who harrassed Job is out to get you!"

The word translated "hath desired" is very strong and implies *successful begging.* So, as in the case of Job, Satan had pleaded for certain liberties with respect to Peter, and evidently his desires had been granted.

It was against this background that Christ prayed for Peter. The term Christ used to describe His act of praying was quite unusual. In fact, it was the first time it had been used in connection with the prayers of Christ. This word gives even greater emphasis to the idea of *petitioning* (asking) with a sense of *need!* Thus Jesus was earnestly asking on behalf of Peter out of a deep sense of need. The grammar also indicates that at the very moment Satan sought permission to spiritually manhandle Peter, Jesus earnestly prayed for him and was successful.

Note, if you will, that Christ's prayer was not that Satan should be prohibited from testing Peter, but rather that "thy faith fail not." Jesus' prayer was that Peter's faith might not utterly collapse. Peter would fall, but not *finally* and *ultimately,* and would come back and strengthen his fellow disciples.

Because Christ deliberately informed Peter of the fact that He had prayed for him, some have tried to argue that the only value in prayer is the inward emotional strength it gives a person. It cannot be denied that there is a legitimate psychological value in knowing that a loved one is praying on our behalf. However, the Bible makes it abundantly clear that it was the fact of Christ's prayer which guaranteed the ultimate security of Peter's faith. The word *But* places Christ's action in direct contrast to Satan's action. Satan actually desired Peter and just as actually, Christ prayed for Peter with the effect that Peter's ultimate victory was assured. It was not the *knowledge* of Satan's intentions toward him that caused Peter's difficulties, so it was not the mere *knowledge* of Christ's prayer that assured ultimate victory. Both Satan's desire and Christ's prayer were equally real.

In this instance, prayer was in the nature of *intercession.* Christ beseeched the Father on behalf of a third party—Peter. Christ prayed specifically for Peter with reference to a *definite, spiritual problem.* He did not vaguely pray, "Father, bless Peter." No! As always, it was precise and *to the point.*

Finally, we can learn from this incident that prayer really works! Peter's faith did not fail for one reason: *Christ prayed.* Exactly how prayer works we are not told (and very frankly I don't think our little minds could handle it even if we were told), but the Bible does clearly tell us that prayer gets the job done.

Prayer for the Holy Spirit: John 14:16. This is not really a record of Christ praying, but a reference to a prayer. In connection with

definite instructions pertaining to new privileges in prayer, He assured
His disciples that He would "pray the Father, and he shall give you
another Comforter . . ." (John 14:16).

The future tense of the verb *pray* makes it evident that this prayer
was as yet historically future. The word *pray* in this instance is not
the normal word used to describe Christ's prayer activity. It literally
means "to ask, to request, or to beseech." Clearly this future prayer
would be petitionary in nature. Christ would ask for "another Comforter, that he may abide with you for ever," and this Comforter is
identified as "the Spirit of truth" (John 14:17).

Christ did not vaguely pray for the future comfort of His disciples
but for a *specific* Comforter to come and accomplish a *precise* task:
Abide with them and be in them forever. This certainly bears little
resemblance to the common, fuzzy generalizations mouthed in the
local prayer meeting.

The effectiveness of Christ's future prayer was already assured
because He went on to say, "He (the Father) shall give you another
Comforter." Do you get the picture? Christ prayed and the Father
gave! The marvelous ministry of the Holy Spirit in this age can be
directly attributed to the power of prayer!

On the Road to Emmaus: Luke 24:30, 31. Now we are on the
victory side of Calvary. Christ has risen! Probably on the same day
of the Resurrection, but late in the afternoon, the risen Lord encoun-
tered two discouraged disciples on the road leading to Emmaus. The
disciples were supernaturally kept from recognizing Him. After chat-
ting with the unrecognized Christ for a while, they invited Him to
share a meal with them. "And it came to pass, as he sat at meat with
them, he took bread, and blessed it, and brake, and gave to them. And
their eyes were opened, and they knew him . . ." (Luke 24: 30, 31).

The phrase "he took bread" indicates that Christ had assumed the
position of host. This was probably true because in the preceding
events on the road, Jesus had very definitely taken the role of Master
and Teacher.

Evidently during the blessing and the distributing of the food, the
eyes of the two disciples "were opened," indicating a supernatural
illumination. Formerly their eyes had been supernaturally "holden"

(Luke 24:16). In both instances, divine activity is implied. Yet most commentators are of the opinion that this divine intervention utilized the manner in which Jesus presided at meals. Something about the way He took and broke the bread, or the way He uttered the prayer-blessing, may well have helped the men recognize Him. The later testimony of these two disciples would seem to bear this out, as they freely acknowledged that Christ was made known to them "in breaking of bread" (Luke 24:35).

Prior to His Ascension: Luke 24:5–53. Luke's writings alone have given us a detailed view of the ascension of our Lord. In this Gospel, Luke makes it plain that Jesus actually engaged in prayer when His ascension took place. The account reads as follows: "And he led them out as far as to Bethany, and he lifted up his hands, and blessed them. And it came to pass, while he blessed them, he was parted from them, and carried up into heaven" (Luke 24: 50, 51).

The prayer on this occasion was a precise act. The root meaning of "blessed" indicates that the nature of this prayer was *praise* rather than petition or intercession. The recipients of the prayer-blessing were "them." So evidently in one act the Lord blessed the entire group. While thus engaged in prayer, the Lord "was parted from them, and carried up into heaven." The language is explicit and clear on this point. It was not immediately after the prayer, but *during the prayer-blessing* that the Lord ascended! If you remember, Christ was actually praying at the initiation of His public ministry (His baptism) and now we are informed that at the conclusion of His public ministry He was also praying. Prayer then characterized both the beginning and the ending of Christ's earthly ministry. It was the alpha and omega.

5
Concluding Thoughts on Christ's Prayer Habits

There can be no question but that the Gospels reveal Christ as the Prince of Pray-ers. With this brief survey of His prayer habits it can safely be said, "Surely never man prayed like this Man." I think it would be of great profit at this point to bring together some of the more significant insights we have gleaned from our study of these instances before proceeding with our investigation.

Crisis more than any other single factor seemed to occasion prayer. When Christ was in trouble His *first* recourse was to pray. I'm sorry to say that with most of us prayer is a *last* resort! Certainly there were other factors that provided occasions for prayer: joy over the report of the seventy, blessing little children, and thankfulness for food. However, His lengthy times of private prayer almost without exception seemed to be provoked by crisis. New crises constituted fresh calls to prayer. Difficulties and emergencies were met only after consultation with the Father in the secret place! I am persuaded that such a practice would make a *significant* difference in the lives of Christians today.

The evidence at this point will not support the pseudo-pious notion that Christ seldom prayed for Himself. *He evidently prayed a great deal for Himself.* To be sure, He prayed for others and their needs, but the evidence indicates much prayer for personal needs. Almost always the indications are that He petitioned for spiritual rather than material needs. Guidance in accomplishing the mission of the Father seems to have been a high-priority item on His prayer list. The glory of the Father was evidently the ultimate motive in all His petitioning.

That Christ's prayers were effective cannot be denied by any serious study of the Gospels. Christ's prayers were always answered. They produced and brought forth powerful, *objective* results. By this I mean prayer actually resulted in benefits to other people. Christ prayed and Lazarus actually arose from the dead. Christ prayed and Peter's faith actually did not fail.

Most amazing are the indications that Christ had complete assurance of answers to prayer before they actually were given. If you will remember, He flatly stated that His prayer concerning Lazarus would be answered before the event took place. Even more astounding is the incident when He confidently announced the answer to a prayer which, as yet, He had not even prayed (*see* John 14:16).

Finally, not only did Christ's prayers produce results but His *prayer example* also brought results. We ought to let folks know if we are earnestly upholding them in prayer. Children will learn the importance of prayer if they actually observe the large and important role it plays in the lives of their parents. Christ's disciples did not need to be told that prayer was important. They *saw* how important it was to their Lord. What do your children see? What do the people in your church see? What do the pupils in your Sunday-school class see?

Modern man may argue, on the basis of his naturalistic presuppositions, against the possibility of prayer as a legitimate force capable of producing real and tangible results in the world of natural law; but all of his arguments are revealed to be nothing more than clanging cymbals, by the serious study of Jesus at prayer.

PART TWO
THE MAJOR PRAYERS OF JESUS

Not only are the prayer habits of Jesus significant in the formulation of a systematic biblical presentation of the doctrine; of even more importance, perhaps, are the actual contents of His prayers. In this section the major prayers of Jesus will be analyzed to discover truths that will help us understand the great subject more fully.

6
The Lord's Prayer

The only extended teaching by Jesus on the subject of prayer is that commonly known as the Lord's Prayer. In reality it is not a prayer which Jesus actually prayed. For example, He never needed to say, "Forgive us our sins," because He was the absolutely sinless One. So strictly speaking, this is a *teaching* prayer. However, because it is a model for prayer, it represents the very highest type of praying. Therefore, we will consider it along with the other major prayers of Christ.

Nature of the Prayer

For hundreds of years the Lord's Prayer has generally been recited in rote fashion. It was so used at the opening session of the World's Parliament of Religions which met in Chicago in 1893. On that occasion, Buddhists, Hindus, Taoists, and other representatives of the great world religions recited the Lord's Prayer in unison!

That Jesus did not intend this prayer to be used in this manner is obvious for several reasons. First, in the setting in which the prayer is found in Luke's account, it is given in response to a request: "Lord, teach us to pray . . ." (Luke 11:1). Clearly the disciples wanted to learn *how* to pray. They did not say, "Lord, teach us a prayer." Second, in Matthew's account, this prayer follows a blast against using vain repetition in prayer (*see* Matthew 6:7). Does it seem likely to you that our Lord would denounce vain repetition and then immediately give a ritual prayer? Third, there is nothing in the grammar by which Christ introduces the prayer that would indicate He intended it to be recited in mechanical fashion. Fourth, the Lord's Prayer was never repeated in the Book of Acts or any New Testament epistle. The Book of Acts contains the account of many early-church prayer meetings, and in some instances records actual prayers, but it never gives the

slightest hint of this prayer being recited. Fifth, so far as we can
determine from church history, the early Christians never used the
Lord's Prayer in their liturgy during the first two hundred years of
the church's existence. Clearly, then, this was a model prayer designed
to teach the disciples the types of things to bring before the Father.
It was never intended to be recited verbatim.

Analysis of the Prayer

The Lord's Prayer contains a brief address plus six well-defined
petitions.

The Address. The prayer begins with a very brief word of address:
"Our Father which art in heaven . . ." (Matthew 6:9). Instantly the
plural nature of the first word *our* strikes us as somewhat unusual.
Why not *my?* The perplexity is heightened when we notice that all
of the pronouns of the prayer are plural. Most Bible teachers are of
the opinion that the plural is used because the believer *always* prays
by virtue of his union with other believers as part of a community or
fellowship. When I pray in private, I pray as part of the body of Christ!
There is a sense in which the body prays when a single member prays!
Thus these plural pronouns serve as a reminder that I, as a believer,
am part of a large brotherhood and I pray as part of that brotherhood.

A clear evidence of this truth can be seen in the fifth petition, "And
forgive us our debts . . ." (Matthew 6:12). Every Christian sins and
needs forgiveness. However, no Christian can ask forgiveness on behalf of another. Each believer must do this for himself! I can't say,
"Father, forgive Susie Smith's sins!" Sister Smith must do that for
herself. Yet, when I ask the Father to forgive my own personal sins,
I actually do the asking, but I ask by virtue of the fact that I'm "in
Christ" and part of the body of Christ.

Thus, our Lord, by the use of plural pronouns, is teaching us that
we are never alone. We never pray, eat, sleep, or work alone. From
God's perspective (which is the realm of reality) we are always viewed
as a group, never as individuals per se! We are individual members
of a body. Christians, you begin to understand this and really believe it, and it will flavor every aspect of your life. You will pray

differently, think differently, work differently, and act differently!

The address is to the Father. If you remember, Christ always addressed His personal prayers to the Father and now, in this model prayer, He is teaching His disciples to address their prayers to the same Person. It should be remembered that Christ spoke in the Aramaic language. Therefore, the word for "Father" which Christ actually used in this case was *Abba*, which could be translated "Daddy" or "Papa."

The word *Abba* denotes intimacy, love, and confidence. Can you imagine what this must have meant to those Jewish disciples? They had been taught not even to pronounce the sacred name Jehovah, and now they were being taught to call out to this God on a "Daddy" basis! Such an idea must have sounded utterly unbelievable.

Before leaving this issue, it should be pointed out that though the word *Abba* denotes intimacy, it also carries the idea of respect. A small child crying out to his father in that day felt love and intimacy toward his parent, but always with an overriding respect. I bring this out because today in our sick culture the concept of Daddy has often lost all connotation of respect. This was not so in the first-century world.

The Petitions. Six petitions form the body of this prayer and actually all six are stated in the form of commands. To phrase a request as a command gives it an urgent impact, one with a sense of decisiveness.

The first petition is "Hallowed be thy name" (Matthew 6:9). I dare say most people view this statement as an expression of adoration or praise. The truth is that it is neither adoration nor praise, but *petition.* Jesus is not teaching us to praise or adore God by this statement, but to ask Him to do something. As stated above, it is given in the form of a command. A literal translation would be, "Cause Your name to be hallowed!"

The verb *hallowed* means "to set apart" or "to sanctify." It carries the idea of treating something as special, above the ordinary. The word *revere* would perhaps be a good contemporary word to convey the essential concept. In this instance the object to be revered is the Father's name. It should be remembered that "name" in biblical times was almost synonymous with the *nature* or *character* of the individual. The request, then, is for God's Person to be revered or esteemed.

The second petition, "Thy kingdom come" (Matthew 6:10), is again in the form of a command. With earnestness and decisiveness, the Father is requested to cause the kingdom to be established. It is not within the scope of this book to argue the nature of the "kingdom" alluded to in this request. It certainly refers to a kingdom to be established fully at some future time. Regardless of one's theological position (amillennialism or premillennialism) virtually every Christian will agree that God's kingdom will not become a full-fledged reality until Christ comes again. All Christians agree that with the full establishment of the kingdom, God's purposes for mankind will have been completed.

So whether or not you think the nature of that fully established kingdom will be spiritual and heavenly or literal and earthly, why not pray for it to come? Why not pray for God's purposes in history to be completed? Is this not the spirit of the early believers at Thessalonica who ". . . turned to God from idols . . . to wait for his Son from heaven . . ." (1 Thessalonians 1:9, 10)?

The third petition, "Thy will be done in earth, as it is in heaven" (Matthew 6:10), is closely associated with the previous request. Its ultimate realization awaits the day when God's purposes in history are fully realized at the coming of Christ. Only then will God's will be fully realized on this old earth where rebellion has prevailed for far too long. As with the previous petitions, this is voiced as a command with great urgency.

The fourth petition, "Give us this day our daily bread" (Matthew 6:11), is very different from the previous three. It is obviously occupied with a matter of personal and practical concern. Thus, at this point, the prayer passes from petitions of aspiration (aspiring to see God's purposes completed) to petitions of personal concern.

While a few try to argue that "bread" should be taken in a spiritual sense, a vast majority of the commentators feel this petition refers to physical bread. Certainly this is the most natural interpretation. Keep in mind that bread was a term that generally covered the idea of food. In this instance we are to petition only for "daily" bread. In all probability "daily" refers to the food needed for a given day.

There is an interesting play on words when one compares Matthew's and Luke's rendering of this petition. Matthew renders it, "Give us *this day* . . ." (Matthew 6:11) while Luke words it, "Give us *day by day* . . ." (Luke 11:3) (author's italics). The main idea in both accounts is the same. Both are prayers for *immediate need*. The way Matthew puts it, we are instructed to pray for *one* day at a time. Luke advances the petition to one extra day's supply; enough for that day and the coming day. The main thing to understand is that neither Matthew nor Luke put forth the thought of praying for a year's supply of food. It is for immediate material need, not a whole truckload of groceries!

The tense of the word *Give* in Matthew indicates decisive, urgent asking, while the tense used by Luke would point up continuous, persistent asking. So putting it all together we have the thought of earnestly and decisively petitioning the Father continuously for our immediate material needs.

Before I leave this petition, let me point out that it is the only specific instance where material needs are mentioned in connection with prayer. As we have observed to this point, Christ is seen praying for spiritual needs.

The fifth petition also pertains to a personal need: "And forgive us our debts, as we forgive our debtors" (Matthew 6:12). The word *debts* in this context refers to the *moral* debts which sinners incur with God when His moral law is violated.

The major thrust of the petition is for forgiveness. Again, the tense and mood of the word indicate decisiveness and urgency. Since this is a prayer lesson given to disciples, the forgiveness can only refer to what might be termed "parental forgiveness," which involves the enjoyment of fellowship between the believer and the Father within God's family. It cannot refer to what might be termed "eternal forgiveness," which pertains to a person's salvation, because these men were already saved individuals.

The petition asks the Father to forgive, "as we forgive our debtors." This phrase has given rise to a great deal of misunderstanding. By some it has been taken to mean that a person is to be forgiven *on the basis* of his forgiveness of others. They insist that today a believer is told to forgive because he has already been forgiven by God's free grace (*see* Ephesians 4:32). So some brothers reject this prayer altogether as having no direct reference to Christians today.

The language of the prayer does not teach that God will forgive us *in kind* based upon the degree to which we forgive others. God never has and never will do this! The word *as* does not indicate *cause*. It does not state the *reason* God should forgive! Note that Jesus did not teach, "Forgive us our debts *because* we forgive our debtors," but *"as* we forgive" (author's italics). There is a difference!

This concept is given even more emphasis when one fully understands the word *forgive*. Matthew uses a tense that indicates an accomplished act and could literally be translated, "as we *did* forgive," the idea being, "Forgive us, Father, in view of the fact that we *have already forgiven.*" It is a *forgiving heart* that seeks and receives God's forgiveness. In order for a disciple to receive "family forgiveness" from the Father, he must himself manifest a forgiving spirit. Now an unforgiving spirit is sin and unacknowledged sin is not forgiven by the Father in this age or any other age. Does not 1 John 1:9 teach us that for a believer to receive forgiveness he must honestly face and acknowledge his sin? In essence that is precisely what this petition is teaching.

The sixth petition, "Lead us not into temptation, but deliver us from evil" (Matthew 6:13), is basically an expression of the correct attitude toward temptation and evil. To welcome temptation is to court disaster. A humility that leads to a complete dependence upon God is the best safeguard against failure in time of trial. There are two definite parts in this petition, separated by a strong word of contrast —*but*.

This petition is not so much a request to be kept from temptations (or testings) as such, but more a plea to be kept from *yielding* when one does experience them. This is made especially clear when both parts of the petition are viewed together. "Don't allow us to yield in time of temptation, *but* (contrast) deliver us from evil." Actually the word translated "evil" is literally "the evil one." It is a reference to Satan who is the active source of such temptations. Prayer is viewed in the New Testament as an aid to making a proper response to testings and temptations! We saw a beautiful example of this earlier in this book. Christ did not pray for Peter not to enter into the testings administered by Satan; rather He prayed that Peter might not ultimately fall while experiencing the temptations.

Doctrinal Implications of the Prayer

We can learn a number of truths concerning praying from this model. The unusual practice of Christ in addressing His prayers to "Father" on an intimate child-parent basis is now advocated for His disciples. I, as a disciple, am hereby instructed to address the God of the universe as Father! If you dwell on how really small and infinitesimal we are and how majestic He is, it really baffles the mind! Yet coupled with the intimacy implied in the word *Father* (Daddy), there is a definite respect because His Person (name) is to be reverently hallowed.

The attitude of the prayer is even more striking. As previously noted, all the petitions are stated in the form of commands and in a verb tense that indicates an attitude of intense urgency. In fact, these petitions are given with the most intense urgency and earnestness that it is possible to convey with Greek grammar. One cannot get the picture of half-interested, detached praying here. Rather the disciples are herein taught to ask with decisiveness and with a sense of fervency.

The nature of the prayer is unquestionably *petitionary.* Except for a brief word of address, the entire model consists of six requests. There is not one direct word of praise, adoration, or thanksgiving in the entire prayer! This prayer is clearly a lesson on how to effectively ask the Father for things.

The six petitions all pertain to *significant issues.* Not one of them is for an obvious triviality. Five of the six petitions pertain basically to *spiritual issues.* This is true even of the request for God's kingdom because, though some of us feel the kingdom will be literal and visible, we would nonetheless concur that it is essentially spiritual in the best usage of that term. So our Lord is trying to teach us to pray primarily for spiritual needs. Does not the entire New Testament teach us that the real battles are in the realm of the spiritual rather than the material? However, the one request for daily bread clearly assures us that it is also perfectly proper to bring immediate material needs to the Father in prayer.

The first three petitions all pertain to the outworking of the Father's purposes on this planet. By implication any prayer request that will hasten the day when God's kingdom will become a reality is this type of petition. Thus praying for your church and your pastor would be this type of petition because of the fact that your church is engaged in activities that will hasten the coming of the kingdom. Likewise, pray for your missionaries.

The final three petitions are all for personal needs, both physical and spiritual. Therefore, I conclude that it is proper to ask the Father for personal needs. The fact that two of the three petitions pertain to spiritual matters should indicate that our most numerous and serious needs are actually in the realm of the spiritual. All too often we seem to feel that our basic problems are such things as jobs, mortgage payments, and disease. Yet God continually tells us that our most numerous and serious problems are in the realm of the spiritual (*see* Ephesians 6:12).

The pattern of this prayer is not really unusual. The petitions begin with God's Person and move to God's program before considering the needs of the individual. However, the order of the three petitions pertaining to the individual are different, to say the least. I think most of us would expect the petition for forgiveness and the request for protection against evil to have been placed before the petition for daily bread. Isn't a person's relationship with God more important than his material needs? The answer is self-evident! Certainly the five-to-one ratio in favor of spiritual needs would rule out any thought of the material needs being preeminent over the spiritual ones. Perhaps this strange order of personal petitions would indicate that the material is important, but by no means all-important!

7
The High Priestly Prayer

The prayer recorded in John 17 is the only long, continuous prayer of Jesus that is preserved for us in the Gospels. This prayer is amazingly simple yet deeply profound. It has been referred to as the most sublime chapter in the Bible. It allows us insight into the very core of the inner life of Jesus Christ.

It is universally recognized basically as a prayer of intercession. The objects of His intercession were His immediate disciples and all future disciples. Usually it is referred to as the High Priestly Prayer, for Christ is seen praying from a perspective that assumes Calvary has already been completed, and that His role of High Priest has been assumed.

Analysis of the Prayer

There is a convenient fourfold division to this great prayer:
(1) Jesus' prayer for Himself: John 17:1–5
(2) Jesus' prayer for His immediate disciples: John 17:6–19
(3) Jesus' prayer for His future disciples: John 17:20–23
(4) Jesus' prayer conclusion: John 17:24–26

Jesus' Prayer for Himself: John 17:1–5. Typically Jesus lifted His eyes heavenward and addressed the prayer to the Father. The request was made because His hour had come. The full expression "the hour is come" (John 17:1) indicates grammatically that the time for His death, burial, Resurrection, and ascension had arrived. This provides a background for the actual request. Oddly enough, the request itself is stated in the *third* person: " . . . glorify thy Son . . ." (verse 1). Putting this petition in common American language we would say, "Father, make Your Son's qualities shine forth and *look good.*" Christ is thereby asking the Father to enable Him to fulfill His ministry, and thus fully accomplish the salvation for which He had come. The verb *glorify* signifies intense urgency. Christ urgently wanted to be glorified!

Now it might sound strange that Christ would ask to be glorified (made to look good), but He quickly gives the reason: " . . . that thy Son also may glorify thee" (verse 1). Plainly Christ did not seek honor here for His own sake! Christ desired to accomplish the work of providing man's salvation in a manner that would make Him *look good,* so it would thereby make the Father whom He represented *look good.* As always, the ultimate goal of all of Christ's praying was the glory of the Father.

In the second and third verses Jesus begins to explain *how* His glorification will ultimately glorify the Father. The Father had given the Son tremendous authority and power in order that by His Crucifixion the Son might give eternal life to men (thus glorifying the Father). The third verse defines the eternal life that Christ had been authorized to give men who come as "knowing" God. The grammar indicates a *continual, growing* acquaintanceship with the Father and the Son. As men really get to intimately know God they cannot help but praise and adore Him. In this manner the Father will be further glorified.

Do you see what Christ has done? He has stated the petition and proceeded to delineate as to *why* He wanted it to be granted, and *how* it would accomplish the desired purpose. All the discussion revolves around the petition.

The second request is made in light of what Christ would shortly accomplish on the cross. Though it is actually stated as if the cross experience had already taken place; by fully and completely accomplishing all that God had sent Him to do, Christ had glorified the Father on the earth (*see* verse 4). This forms a basis or rationale for His second appeal, the sense being, "Father, in view of the fact that I've accomplished all of this, I now have a second request to make."

Our Lord's second petition is voiced once again in a mood and tense that indicates an issue of pressing importance. He cries out, "And now, O Father, glorify thou me . . ." (verse 5). The word emphasized in the request is *now.* Christ wants this and He wants it right away.

To make the request even more emphatic, He says, "Glorify thou me. . . ." Christ is not asking for anyone else, but for *Himself* to be glorified in this request.

Next He specifies exactly the type of glory He desires: ". . . with the glory which I had with thee before the world was" (verse 5). Christ, in becoming a man, had voluntarily chosen not to utilize certain divine characteristics. He did this to fully identify with man so He could redeem us. Now that redemption has been accomplished, He desires restoration of all He had previously laid aside. Study this request in light of Philippians 2:5–11. Notice how very specific Christ is in voicing His petitions!

Jesus' Prayer for His Immediate Disciples: John 17:6–19. The Lord now moves from petitioning on behalf of Himself to intercession on behalf of His eleven disciples. He voices two requests, carefully delineating His reasoning behind such petitions.

The disciples are first described according to their relationship to the Father ("thine they were") and to the Son ("thou gavest them me"), and then according to what they had done with the message of Christ (verse 6).

In the next main thought, our Lord continues to identify the disciples, particularly with reference to the vast amount of instruction that had been communicated to them. These men knew all things which the Father had given to Christ. Evidently they had advanced to the point of understanding that the character and labors of Christ were really coming from the Father (*see* verse 7). In fact, progress can be seen in their reception of His instructions. First, they had "received" the words. Second, they had "known" that Christ came from God, then they had "believed" that God had sent Christ (verse 8).

The purpose of this lengthy report is to impress the Father with the fact that these disciples had been carefully prepared and were fully qualified to represent Him on the earth. This would add incentive to the request He would shortly make on their behalf. It is intended as a buildup to the petition, the idea being, "Father, this is no ordinary group of men I am praying for! They are special and, therefore, it is crucial that My request on their behalf be granted."

Christ next indicates specifically the group for whom He is praying:

"I pray for them" (verse 9). The grammar indicates that this designation is both personal and emphatic. Christ wanted to leave absolutely no doubt as to the identity of the group for whom He was petitioning.

As if this were not enough, He adds the statement "I pray not for the world . . ." (verse 9). Christ wants the Father to know that at the present moment He only has the eleven disciples in mind rather than all mankind. This statement should not be pushed to mean that Christ *never* prayed for anyone other than His disciples. In fact, we have two definite occasions when the Gospels record Him praying for people who were not His disciples (*see* Matthew 19:13 and Luke 18:15). However, the evidence does indicate that Christ prayed almost exclusively for His own followers and very little for the world.

Christ proceeds to delineate the reason He singled out the eleven for prayer. It was because they belonged to God and were the chosen medium for reaching the world (*see* verse 10). They needed prayer since Christ was soon going to leave them and return to His Father. This would mean that they would be left "in the world" (verse 11). In this context the word *world* means the world of unsaved men and the society, culture, and values that they have established. It is the world over which Satan rules as the prince and the power of the air. Therefore, *an intense need existed for the request Christ was about to make!*

Are you getting the significance of all this? One almost gets the impression that Christ is trying to convince the Father of the crucial necessity of granting the request, and in a reverent sense that is exactly what He is doing. In light of this, how can some men portray prayer as simply "conversation with God"?

As might be expected in this context of serious need, the actual petition is stated in a manner indicating that the matter was important, pressing, and serious: ". . . Holy Father, keep through thine own name those whom thou hast given me . . ." (verse 11). Christ's desire is for the Father to keep these disciples from evil. The verb *keep* is used in the sense of "protective oversight."

The reason for thus guarding and keeping the disciples is clearly stated: ". . . that they may be one, as we are" (verse 11). This oneness was in some manner to reflect the intimate unity existing between the

Father and the Son. Though our minds may not fully comprehend all that is involved in these words, it is again evident that Christ was very specific in what He wanted the Father to do.

The actual request is followed by extensive explanation and elucidation. While Christ was in the world He had supernaturally protected the disciples by power given Him by the Father. Except for the special situation involving Judas, not one of them was lost. From now on, however, Christ Himself would no longer be with them and thus other protection was necessary (*see* verse 12). He mentions for the second time His forthcoming departure because this was the occasion for the entire prayer (*see* verse 13).

The Satan-controlled world system was alien to the eleven and actually hated them. However, the disciples had a great work to accomplish! They had been given God's word and had to preach it to a needy world. (*See* v. 14.) Thus Christ once more attempts to convince the Father of the crucial necessity of granting the petition! Prior to stating the petition, He had done much the same thing, as we have seen. Now, after stating the petition, He's still trying to impress the Father with the significance of the issue! It's evident that prayer, for Christ, does not consist of stating a bare list of petitions. In a sanctified sense He not only states the petition but also attempts to convince the Father by showing Him how important it is!

Christ next proceeds to *clarify* the petition He had initially stated in verse eleven: "I pray not that thou shouldest take them out of the world, but that thou shouldest keep them from the evil" (verse 15). The thought is, "Father, when I previously petitioned You to protect them, I did not thereby request their removal from this world, but their protection while in it." After all, the disciples had a job to do on this earth, so our Lord makes sure the Father understands exactly what He meant by the petition.

Do you see how all of the lengthy conversation of verses 6–15 has revolved around the single petition of verse eleven? This has not been aimless conversation but conversation with a purpose. It has consisted of explanation, elucidation, and clarification with reference to that single petition. Remove the petition and the entire discussion becomes meaningless!

Now our Lord gets ready to present a new petition by once again repeating the statement made earlier in verse fourteen: "They are not of the world . . ." (verse 16). This forms the ground (or necessity) for the request for sanctification.

The actual request, "Sanctify them . . ." (verse 17), is voiced once again with the mood and tense that indicates intense urgency. The word *sanctify* carries the root idea of "to set apart God and holy purposes." Thus Christ intently petitions the Father that the eleven be set apart and equipped for their God-ordained mission in the world.

He specifies that the sanctification be accomplished "through thy truth" (verse 17). The "word" could either be a reference to Christ Himself or to the sacred Scriptures. Because the Bible infallibly presents the Person and teachings of Christ, the "word" could possibly be a reference to both. The "truth" of Christ is enshrined in the "word" of Scripture. There the disciple learns what God requires and how He allows him to fulfill the requirements, thus enabling sanctification to take place. The reason the disciples would desperately need this special sanctification by the word was that they were to be sent out "into the world" (verse 18). They needed to be equipped!

In some sense our Lord deemed it necessary to sanctify Himself (*see* verse 19). Certainly Christ did not need to make Himself holy, but evidently He did need to consecrate (devote) Himself to completing His mission. The words "for their sakes" make it evident that this special self-sanctification was necessary in some way to make the disciples' sanctification possible. Exactly how His sanctification would make theirs possible we are not told. Perhaps Christ devoting Himself to completing His mission would enable His disciples to have His example as well as His message to proclaim. Also, the power derived from His sacrifice would allow them to effectively proclaim it.

The important thing for our study is to once again notice how precisely the request is stated and the lengths to which our Lord went to support the need for the request to be granted. There is clearly the element of struggle and persuasion in this prayer.

Jesus' Prayer for His Future Disciples: John 17:20–23. The remaining portion of the prayer broadens in scope to include not only the eleven disciples but also all who would believe through their word. He does not voice any new petitions for them. Rather He includes them in the two petitions He had previously made for the eleven.

The phrase "That they all may be one . . ." expresses the *reason* or *purpose* of the petition rather than the content (verse 21).

In verse 20 when Christ says, "Neither pray I for these alone . . ." He intends for us to understand that the petitions He had previously voiced on behalf of the eleven disciples (*see* verses 11 and 17) should also be applied to all future disciples who would believe "through their word" (verse 20). This enables all disciples to be one (*see* verse 21). Thus Christ never actually asks the Father to *make* all believers one, but rather prays that all believers might be kept in God's name (*see* verse 11), and sanctified in God's truth (*see* verse 17), so that "they all may be one" (verse 21). Unity is assured if the two petitions are granted.

The reason unity among believers was so crucial is next stated: ". . . that the world may know that thou hast sent me . . ." (verse 23). So unity is directly related to evangelism.

Beyond question, Christ is interested in the salvation of lost men. Yet He does not pray directly for their salvation! Rather He prays *directly* for His own disciples so that lost men might be saved and in this way is praying *indirectly* for unbelievers. There is a difference!

Jesus' Prayer Conclusion: John 17:24–26. Along with many commentators, I look upon these verses as an epilogue or conclusion to this beautiful prayer of Jesus.

As is the case with verse 20, some look upon the statement "Father, I will that they also . . . be with me where I am . . ." (verse 24), as a final prayer petition. However, the grammar is entirely out of character with the way our Lord uniformly voices His petitions. The words *I will* could easily be translated "I wish." They are stated as a simple fact rather than a request. The wish is twofold: first, that believers should be with Him; second, that believers should behold His glory. This glory was the heavenly glory which He had before His incarnation and which He had prayed to be restored to Him in verse five.

Addressing God as "righteous Father" (verse 25), our Lord closes the prayer with a benediction. The Lord contrasts the knowledge that the world has of the Father with that which He has. The world does not know God but Christ does and His disciples recognize that fact (*see* verse 25). Jesus had revealed the Father to the disciples and would continue to do so in order that God's mighty love might be communicated to them (*see* verse 26).

Doctrinal Implications of the Prayer

Certainly this prayer is loaded with important implications. The now typical address "Father" was not only practiced but emphasized as well. Three of the four petitions were addressed directly to "Father."

After a brief initial statement of fact, "Mine hour is come" (*see* verse 1), the Lord launched immediately into a petition. The lack of introductory words of praise or thanksgiving is rather startling. The impression is that Christ moved directly into the business of asking the Father to grant certain requests.

If we understand that intercession is a special type of petition, it becomes apparent that the primary nature of this prayer is petitionary. The purpose of this prayer was essentially to ask the Father for things! All of the conversational elements are inseparably tied in with the four petitions. The petitions are uniformly urgent in character. Our Lord was indeed in earnest as He voiced this prayer.

The petitions are stated in specific terminology. There is no hint of generality or vagueness. Christ knew exactly what he desired of the Father and clearly defined His requests. When He asked for glory, in each case He carefully distinguished precisely what kind of glory He desired. When He asked for His own to be kept, He carefully enumerated exactly what was meant by that request. Christ not only asked for specific items but in each case He also backed up the requests with sound reasoning designed to show the importance and need of those specific requests being granted.

Christ was likewise specific with respect to those for whom He prayed. He made it plain that the petitions at first pertained only to the immediate disciples and not to mankind in general. Later He broadened the scope of His prayer to include a larger group, but still was explicit as to whom that larger group would include.

Christ's petitions were all for spiritual benefits. This is most significant in the case of His petitions on behalf of His own disciples. These men were going to be called upon to spearhead world evangelism. They had virtually nothing by way of financial resources. Certainly we might have expected the Lord to petition for some sort of financial assistance for these evangelists. I dare say that issue would occupy a large part of our praying in similar circumstances today. Yet our Lord asked *exclusively* for their spiritual protection and sanctification!

Not only did Christ's petitions pertain exclusively to spiritual matters but they also were all for *significant* matters. This simply reinforces our previous observations that Christ never engaged in prayer trivialities. These requests were for significant spiritual items which were desperately needed.

Perhaps the most interesting element in this prayer is its extensive conversational tone. Out of twenty-six verses, it can be said conservatively that twenty-one of them are set in a motif of earnest conversation with the Father. Up to this point, conversation has not played a significant role in Christ's praying.

Does this prayer, with its extended conversational context, validate the theory that prayer is essentially conversation? The answer must be a categorical *no!* A close study of the conversational material will reveal that it pertains directly to four petitions. The conversation consists of argumentation, explanation, and elucidation pertaining to the requests! This prayer is not general conversation but conversation with a purpose; and more accurately, with a *petitionary purpose!* Remove the petitions and the conversation would be meaningless!

However, once the function of the large conversational element is seen in its proper perspective, it becomes even more significant. Christ evidently felt it necessary not only to voice petitions to the Father but also to enter into lengthy and elongated discussions as to *why* the petition was given, *what* the petition involved, and the *ultimate purpose* He had in mind in voicing the petition. To be sure, a certain amount of this explanatory material can be attributed to the fact that the prayer was voiced out loud in the hearing of the disciples, and for their benefit. Yet the deep ring of urgency, sincerity, and intimacy throughout the prayer argues that Christ was not simply explaining these petitions solely for the benefit of the listening disciples. The human Jesus evidently felt compelled to explain to the Father in detail the importance and reasons for His requests.

Noticeably lacking in this prayer is any hint of confession of sin on the part of the Lord, and this is to be expected of the One who knew no sin. What is *not* expected is the lack of any extensive sections devoted explicitly to such matters as praise, adoration, or thanksgiving! To be sure, such elements are present in the prayer. They are interwoven throughout the prayer in the explanatory material, but in an almost offhand manner. This most certainly presents a different approach to prayer. Yet this is precisely what is found!

The intensely personal nature of the prayer should be evident even to the most casual reader. This is obviously not a prayer offered to an abstract deity in formal language. It is to one whom Jesus knew intimately and personally as Father!

The motive in the petitions is the *ultimate glory of God!* The ground of the entire prayer is the furtherance of God's glory by the accomplishment of His purposes on the earth.

History has verified that God truly answered this prayer of Christ by the phenomenal success of those early disciples against overwhelming odds. On the day of Pentecost the Holy Spirit did actually indwell all believers. Today every believer is spiritually and actually one with Christ! By that same Spirit all believers are preserved until their redemption is complete. Today fullness of joy is available to every believer. The love of God is poured out in the hearts of believers by that same Holy Spirit! In fact, the only part of the prayer that awaits fulfillment is the Lord's final wish that all believers might someday behold His glory!

8
The Prayer in Gethsemane

Certainly no other prayer incident in the earthly life of the Lord displays the degree of grief and emotional tension that is herein observed. It seems highly probable that the author of the Book of Hebrews referred to the Gethsemane experience when he wrote, "In the days of his flesh, Jesus offered up prayers and supplications, with loud cries and tears, to him who was able to save him from death, and he was heard for his godly fear" (Hebrews 5:7 RSV).

Analysis of the Prayer

A short distance inside the garden, Jesus told His disciples to sit down while He proceeded farther into the garden. Christ's purpose for proceeding deeper into the garden was to go and pray yonder (*see* Matthew 26:36).

As our Lord proceeded deeper into the garden, accompanied by His three closest disciples, His inner anguish became increasingly apparent. Matthew describes it in these words: "He . . . began to be sorrowful and very heavy" (verse 37). The word *began* indicates the commencement of a new level of sorrow more severe in degree than our Lord had ever experienced before!

Jesus' new emotional state is described as "sorrowful" by Matthew or "sore amazed" by Mark (14:33), which in this instance carries the idea of *sorrow to the point of great amazement.* One could almost translate it by the word *terrified!* Our Lord had for a long time foreseen the time of His passion. He had, on numerous occasions, predicted it. Yet when it now came clearly into view its terrors exceeded the anticipations of the human Jesus and *terrified* Him!

Following the amazed and terrified shock, our Lord's condition is said to be "very heavy" (Matthew 26:37). Again, the word is extremely potent! It describes a confused, restless, half-distracted state —the distress following great shock! Some scholars are of the opinion that this emotional shock must have affected His actual physical appearance. Our Lord was visibly shaken. Evidently it was at this time that the awareness of Calvary and all it involved came in upon the human Jesus with a traumatic, terrifying jolt which left Him extremely disturbed. The words *sore amazed* and *very heavy* combine to depict a serious emotional state which was evident in the very facial expression of the Lord. Remember that though Christ was 100 percent God, He had at this point laid aside His glory and was functioning as a man! The humanity of Jesus is very evident in His praying.

In this serious emotional state, Christ bared His feelings verbally to the three disciples: "My soul is exceeding sorrowful, even unto death . . ." (verse 38). In every conceivable manner the Bible describes Christ in a drastic state of emotional distress. He had reached an extremity of anguish that was approaching the utmost limit of endurance. Not one of us has even approached such a degree of inner trauma.

In this intensely troubled state, Jesus requested the three disciples to remain at that spot and "watch" (verse 38). The tense of the verb indicates He intended them to continuously remain awake, in order to warn of any approaching danger. Notice He did not ask them to pray for or with Him in this time of distress. However, Luke lets us know that Jesus did urge these men to pray for themselves lest they should enter temptation (*see* Luke 22:40).

Thus in an alarming state of emotional strain Jesus deliberately sought solitude in order to pray. In this instance He even seemed to take extraordinary precaution to guarantee an undisturbed session of prayer. Do you really see the impact of all this? Though His emotional state was so extreme it was visible on His very countenance, and though He was clearly aware of the horrible events coming in the next few hours, Jesus did not ask even His closest human associates to pray for Him. However, prayer was essential in this crisis, and the Incarnate Christ proceeded to do just that!

Christ's First Prayer Retreat: Matthew 26:39–41. Luke uses a very strong phrase "was withdrawn" (Luke 22:41), to indicate that something actually forced Christ onward to prayer. Some experts feel it was the very force of His emotions that drove Him. After being withdrawn a short distance Jesus "fell on his face" (Matthew 26:39). Mark uses a verb tense that indicates repeated or continuous action (*see* Mark 14:35). Christ was in such emotional anguish that He repeatedly threw Himself to the ground! To say the least the language indicates a desperate struggle. It is beyond question the most graphic portrait yet presented of the titanic struggle of the soul involved in the Lord's prayer life. Friend, this is a picture of struggle, not tranquility! This is battle, not beatitude! We cannot even begin to imagine the anguish and intensity involved in this prayer scene.

All three Gospel writers indicate continuous action in prayer. There can be no doubt that this first prayer session was far more lengthy than the recorded petition, "O my Father, if it be possible, let this cup pass from me: nevertheless not as I will, but as thou wilt" (Matthew 26:39). The petition recorded in verse 39 is simply a sample that represents the major thrust of a lengthy prayer.

Christ's usual prayer address was simply "Father," but in this instance Jesus cried with tremendous emotion by saying, "My Father," reaching up as closely as possible to His Father's heart.

The first petition begins with the phrase "If it be possible . . ." (verse 39). The grammar indicates that there was no question in Christ's mind of the Father's ability. Our Lord was fully confident that He was able to cause the cup to pass from Him. It was not a question of God's ability but of His will! Luke emphasizes this aspect by stating the same idea in different words: "If thou be willing . . ." (Luke 22:42).

The actual request was in the form of an urgent command: "Let this cup pass from me" (Matthew 26:39). The request was to escape from the cup. *Cup* was used figuratively in the Old Testament for God's wrath (*see* Psalms 75:8). Virtually all commentators agree that the word *cup* in this instance refers to the cross and all the anguish that would be involved in it, both physical and spiritual. Certainly the chief horror in the mind of Christ was the thought of being made sin on behalf of you and me!

Some find it difficult to conceive of Christ ever making such a request. Didn't Christ know the Father's will? But it must be remem-

bered that Jesus voiced this petition under almost unimaginable emotional stress. Also, in prayer the humanity of Christ is always in the
forefront. The Incarnate Christ was pure deity, but it was a *self-
emptied deity*. Christ had laid aside His glory in becoming a man.
Clearly the Gospels reveal instances when Jesus did not know some
things during His life on earth. Thus an emotional outburst of such
a nature is very typically human even for one of the stature of Jesus
Christ! Very possibly our Lord in His incarnate state was not altogether certain of what the Father under the circumstances might
think best.

However, one thing is clear: Christ desired the Father's will above
all else. He concluded His request by saying, "Nevertheless not as I
will, but as thou wilt" (verse 39). Luke makes it even more graphic
by phrasing it, "Nevertheless not my will, but thine, be done" (Luke
22:42). Luke alone records that after this titanic prayer struggle, an
angel strengthened Christ (*see* Luke 22:43). Again, the emphasis is
upon the *human* Jesus because pure deity would never need such
angelic help.

Our Lord then returned to His disciples. He awakened them and
urged them to pray for themselves in order that they would not enter
into temptation. Notice the difference if you will. Christ prayed to be
spared from the cup but urged them to pray to be spared the trials
which their association with Him would involve. As events proved,
it was not the Father's will to spare either Christ or the disciples. Yet
lack of prayer deprived the disciples of the victory which Christ,
through prayer, won that night. Clearly the victory of Jesus was won
through petitionary prayer. The disciples were deprived of a similar
victory because they failed to pray.

Christ's Second and Third Prayer Retreats: Matthew 26:42–44.
When the Lord returned to the place of prayer after awakening His
sleeping disciples, Luke reports Him to be in a condition of *agony*
(*see* Luke 22:44). This word occurs only here in the New Testament.
It is used to describe the climax of the mysterious soul conflict and
unspeakable suffering of our Lord. The root idea is taken from the
struggle and pain of an athletic contest. The full expression, "being
in an agony" (Luke 22:44), conveys the idea of growing intensity.

Christ had progressed in struggle from the first prayer into an even more intensive combat. The intensity of this anguish is again heightened by the fact that Christ is said to have "sweat . . . as it were great drops of blood . . ." (verse 44). Vocabulary fails to depict adequately the emotional agony of this moment. Yet in this intense emotional state "he prayed" (verse 44). Deep emotions not only prompted prayer, but earnest prayer, for Luke adds that Jesus prayed "more earnestly." Heightened emotional distress produced heightened prayer effort! Jesus literally prayed hardest when it was hardest to pray!

Only Matthew gives us a hint as to what words were said in the second prayer session: "O my Father, if this cup may not pass away from me, except I drink it, thy will be done" (Matthew 26:42). Clearly this second prayer shows an advance upon the first. It is as though the Lord had made up His mind that the cup could *not* pass from Him. The address is exactly the same ("my Father"), but the content of the petition is quite different. This time He states the condition in the form of a negative: "If this cup may *not* pass away from me . . ." (author's italics). He knows that it is not possible, yet the human Jesus seems to wish that it were!

The Lord continues His request with another conditional clause: ". . . except I drink it. . . ." This clause expresses *probability.* In fact, it expresses a high degree of probability. Thus the first clause was assumed to be true (the cup could not pass away), but the second clause expresses the thought that it was quite apparent that Christ would drink the cup. Obviously Christ was now realizing the absolute will of God and was beginning to face up emotionally to the fact that He would actually drink the cup. The delicate distinction between the two conditional clauses displays the *real* attitude of Jesus toward the subtle temptation of bypassing Calvary.

Again, this second session ends with the same earnest petition: "Thy will be done." So in both prayer sessions Christ concludes with a cry of submission to the Father's will. However, grammar indicates in this second session that His intensity is heightened due to His overwhelming desire to do His Father's will.

The third time Christ prayed, Matthew simply records that He "prayed the third time, saying the same words" (verse 44). The "same words" could possibly mean that Christ voiced the same *sentiment* and *substance* as He did in the previous prayers. It would not necessarily mean the same words. Does this not give us an interesting commentary on Christ's earlier teaching about "vain repetitions" (Matthew 6:7)? It certainly demonstrates that it is legitimate to bring the same request over and over again to the Father. It can certainly be said that repeated earnest petitions are to be distinguished from *vain* repetitions.

At any rate, the specific request that the cup be removed was not granted, for it was not in conformity to the Father's will. However, the overall prayer was answered in that the primary consideration throughout was, "Thy will be done." So the prayer *was* answered because it is a matter of record that Christ was indeed fully submissive to divine will! In fact, shortly after this incident when Judas perpetrated His betrayal, our Lord said, "Shall I not drink the cup which the Father has given me?" (John 18:11 RSV.)

I cannot help but be impressed with the tremendous contrast between the emotional state of our Lord when He entered the garden that night and when He left in chains to be tried and crucified. Throughout the entire course of the arrest and trial, Jesus was the picture of a man on top of the situation. He displayed tranquility in the midst of turbulence. Something obviously happened in the garden that radically changed the emotional condition of Jesus. *Through prayer* an emotionally disturbed Christ left the garden with quiet confidence to accomplish the Father's will. Certainly, if nothing else, Gethsemane serves as a practical example of the Lord's own admonition: "Men ought always to pray, and not to faint" (Luke 18:1).

Doctrinal Implications of the Prayer

There are many factors concerning prayer that are by now familiar. Christ entered that garden with one purpose in mind—to pray! Once more it was a crisis that prompted prayer. Often we have seen Christ's desire for seclusion in prayer. In this instance He demanded it! As noted, this secluded spot was probably a habitual place of prayer for our Lord.

Of unusual significance is the attention given in the account to the physical position Christ assumed while praying. More attention is given to this issue in this account than any of the others. Luke records Christ simply as kneeling; Matthew pictures Him as prostrate upon the ground, and Mark says He repeatedly fell to the ground! Putting all three together, Christ probably first fell to His knees and as the agony intensified, He literally prostrated Himself. Then, in the height of the prayer struggle, He was in such torment of soul that He was literally writhing in anguish upon the ground. In all probability neither the kneeling nor the prostration were the normal positions Christ assumed while praying. Their very mention and emphasis in this account argues that such behavior appeared unusual to the disciples. They probably had never seen Him conduct Himself in such fashion before. Actually the account indicates that the emotional agony of soul caused Christ to end up prostrate upon the ground. By that I mean He did not assume the kneeling or prostrate positions in order to pray (or even in order to pray more effectively), but rather our Lord, oblivious to His physical position in the intensity of His prayer battle, ended up prostrate upon the ground!

The prayer address is a little unusual, but completely appropriate under the circumstances. The language of this prayer pictures a small child crying out in desperation to His daddy in the most intimate language possible!

Though the three recorded prayers are of short duration, the sleeping disciples indicate a lengthy session. After all, the disciples would hardly have had time to fall asleep if the sessions consisted only of what is recorded! Each time Christ returned from a session, He found the disciples fast asleep. What is recorded is only the major thrust of what Christ was seeking from the Father.

The purpose of the sessions was precise and definite. Jesus did not pray because it was a certain hour of the day or a certain day of the week. He did not pray because He felt that as a pious Jew He was obligated to spend a certain amount of time in such activity! Obviously, Christ engaged in prayer as specific needs arose and for precise purposes!

Though just a little of the actual prayer is retained for us, the sampling we do have is definitely and *exclusively* petitionary in nature!

In each instance our Lord launches immediately into petition after the address "My Father." There is no direct praise, thanksgiving, or adoration. Not one prayer of Christ can be cited that demonstrates the popular notion that "nice" prayers must consist of a balance of adoration, confession, thanksgiving, and supplication (the so-called ACTS formula for prayer)! When Christ praised, He praised! When He thanked, He thanked! When He petitioned, He petitioned!

Beyond question the most dramatic aspect of this prayer session was the emotional context. It arose out of an intensely troubled spirit. The language indicates emotional strain comparable to that of athletes in agonizing combat. The turmoil was so fierce that His face was twisted unnaturally.

During the session the distress heightened, which simply motivated Christ to even more intense prayer. The prayer battle reached the point where it was physically manifested in the form of a bloody sweat! Now let's face it. When a man does that He's praying with feeling! He's praying with intensity!

As one would expect in such a highly charged context, the petitions were voiced with a sense of burning importance demanding immediate attention. All of the petitions were for Christ Himself! He did not pray for His disciples or anyone else in this prayer. The idea that good praying must include intercession for others before a person prays for himself cannot be substantiated here. However, it is obvious that Christ's overriding desire was to glorify the Father, as is evidenced in the often repeated "Thy will be done." Beyond doubt this provides the finest example of the basic underlying consideration which governed all of Christ's praying. Regardless of personal inconvenience Christ desired the Father's will, even if it meant drinking the awful cup.

Of special interest is the fact that Jesus repeated the same basic request at least three times, if not more. This will do much to further our understanding of what really constitutes a "vain repetition."

The evidence is clear that prayer produced results. Christ was in a markedly different emotional state after the prayer session. He entered the garden visibly disturbed and in deep anguish of soul. He left the garden in command of the situation. He remained controlled and calm throughout the ordeal of arrest and trial. Why? Because He

prayed! By contrast, the disciples failed to pray and when the crunch came, they folded and fled. Prayer made the difference!

Christ in Gethsemane certainly furnishes a living example of His own teaching, to the effect that "Men ought always to pray, and not to faint." Friend, when the going gets rough, don't fold—pray!

9
The Prayers From the Cross

The last major prayers of Christ were those which He uttered while hanging upon the cross. Seven recorded utterances poured from His soul during that ordeal. Three of these can be classified as prayer. First Christ prayed for His persecutors and then for Himself. He then prayed as He presented His soul to the Father. As would be expected, they were all highly emotional outbursts.

The Prayer for His Persecutors: Luke 23:34. After His executioners nailed Him to the cross, Luke records that Jesus cried, "Father, forgive them; for they know not what they do" (Luke 23:34). Virtually all agree that this prayer was uttered very early in the crucifixion process. Some feel these could have been the very first words our Lord said while hanging upon the cross. Others are of the opinion that the prayer was actually said at that terrible moment when the Saviour was stretched out upon the cross and the nails were being driven through the palms of His hands.

Analysis of the Prayer

The petition "Forgive them" is voiced in a manner typical of Jesus' prayer practice. It is given in a mood and tense that indicates that Christ considered this petition of pressing importance. A man in the process of being crucified would hardly pray about issues he considered trivial. The reason for the petition is next stated by the phrase ". . . for they know not. . . ." The problem was ignorance in what they were doing. This appeal was on behalf of those actually engaged in the Crucifixion. It was the Roman soldiers who were ignorant of their actions. So far as they were concerned it was simply another execution. However, the Jewish officials and the populace of Jerusalem who shouted, "Away with Him!" knew what they were doing.

Doctrinal Implications of the Prayer

This prayer demonstrates once more the appropriateness of spontaneous emotional outbursts as needs arise. It is a classic example of Paul's admonition about "continuing instant in prayer" (Romans 12:12). We ought to be so programmed that all during the day as needs arise prayer is given right on the spot. So often we slug through the problems of the day and only rarely, as a last resort, do we cry out to God in prayer. Prayer ought to be a first resort! Even in the anguish of Calvary, Christ was aware of the spiritual needs of others. Notice that amid the pain and turmoil, Christ was still careful to explain to the Father the *reason* for making the request! This feature has been typical of all of Christ's prayers, and its presence at this point seems to indicate a fixed habit. A man having nails driven through his hands would hardly be expected to pray for others in the first place, much less to state a reason for making the request! But Jesus was not in the habit of rattling off a string of bare petitions the way we would read a grocery list. He always stated reasons and evidently this fixed habit prevailed even in this unlikely context.

What is most unusual about this prayer is the fact that it represents one of the few times that Jesus prayed for unsaved people! His general rule seems to have been, "I pray not for the world . . ." (John 17:9). This prayer was not a prayer for the eternal salvation of His persecutors, but rather a prayer with reference to a specific act in which they were ignorantly engaged.

The Prayer for Himself: Matthew 27:46; Mark 15:34. The words of this emotional outburst are actually a quotation of the first verse of the Twenty-Second Psalm. Christ was so saturated with the Word of God that in that time of terrible distress He actually prayed the words of the Psalm. Of course, I believe that David wrote the Psalm prophetically, and that Christ upon this occasion was simply fulfilling Old Testament prophecy. This was the heartfelt cry of the Lamb of God bearing the sin of the world. Of all the statements from the cross it is the most profound and difficult. These are the only words from the cross recorded by Matthew and Mark. Both record this prayer in the Aramaic: "Eli, Eli, la ma sabach tha ni?" The Greek translation would be, "My God, my God, why hast thou forsaken me?" (Matthew 27:46).

Setting of the Prayer

This cry was uttered about three o'clock in the afternoon (*see* Matthew 27:45). Jesus had been hanging from the cross for many hours. He had been scoffed at by the multitudes, the Sanhedrin, the soldiers, and even by the two robbers on either side of Him. For the three hours immediately preceding this outcry the entire scene had been shrouded in total blackness. Shortly after this pathetic cry, death came to our Lord. It represents depths of anguish which no mortal can ever fully appreciate.

Analysis of the Prayer

The first word, *And,* ties in the anguished cry with the total darkness mentioned in the preceding verse (45). The three hours of total darkness were a sign from God witnessing to the unusual nature of this event. So in connection with this great sign, Jesus shouted forth in prayer. That a climax of torment had been reached is also indicated by the tone of Jesus' voice. It was not a whisper or a monotone but a *loud cry.* Thus all indications point to a degree of agony even exceeding that of Gethsemane.

In this agonized state, Jesus cried, "My God, my God, why hast thou forsaken me?" The words *My God* are actually one word in the Greek, and the use of them is the only instance of that form of the word *God* ever being used in the New Testament. The idea is that Jesus was *directly* addressing God.

It is also the only record where Jesus addressed His Father by the word *God* when He prayed. Why He departed from His fixed habit we cannot be sure. Was it the intense agony? Was it tied in with the mysterious separation between Father and Son? Was it because at that moment Jesus was bearing human sin? At any rate, this was not our Lord's normal prayer address. Though the address was not the intimate filial "Father" it was far from impersonal because of the word *my.* It was not "God, God," but "My God, My God!" Likewise the word *God* reminds us of the same submission to divine will as voiced in the anguish of the garden. Even though the Father, in some manner unexplainable to our human minds, had turned from Him in the awful darkness, Jesus cried to Him as *His God.* Certainly this is an indication of human-divine perfection. In short, He was a Lamb without spot or blemish.

The word *why* indicates purpose, the idea being, "For what purpose have You forsaken Me?" This prayer is not a petition or an intercession, but rather a question. Evidently Christ, emptied of certain divine glories, did not understand the purpose of this awful forsaking as it pertained to providing human salvation. Indeed, it is hidden from us today! About all we can say is that only by such a forsaking could our complete redemption be accomplished.

The divine separation is described by the word *forsaken,* which carries the idea of deserting someone in a set of circumstances that are against him. In plain American "slanguage" we would use terms such as "let down, desert, abandon, or leave in the lurch." Some Bible teachers try to soften the concept to mean, "to leave helpless." They contend that it does not indicate the Father withdrew His *Person* from Christ, but simply His *help!*

We do not fully understand why Jesus cried out! This is probably one of the most difficult areas for the Bible scholar to handle. All seem to connect this agonizing separation with the consciousness Christ must have had of being the world's Sin Bearer (*see* 2 Corinthians 5:21). Our human minds cannot probe beyond the fact that in some way, for an awful moment, even the love of the Father seems to have been withdrawn from Him. For this present study the point is that in the precise moment of agony, Jesus cried out in *prayer.* He did not faint, *He prayed!*

Doctrinal Implications of the Prayer

Though all recognize this as a legitimate prayer, it differs in a marked manner from all other prayers of Jesus. It departs from our Lord's normal address ("Father"), but as already seen it nevertheless maintains a real sense of intimacy with the address "My God." This prayer also departs from Christ's general habit of petitioning in prayer. In this case He is asking a question. Thus it demonstrates that prayer content can include a great variety of elements. It can include thanksgiving, praise, intercession, petitions, and questions!

The effective nature of this prayer outburst is implied by Christ's final statement from the cross: "Father, into thy hands I commend my spirit" (Luke 23:46). The implication seems to be that though no petition was made verbally, this agonizing question was at the same time a cry for aid and relief which the Father graciously answered.

The Prayer for His Presentment: Luke 23:46. It is generally conceded that this prayer followed closely the preceding emotional outburst. Jesus' cry, "My God, my God, why hast thou forsaken me?" (Matthew 27:46) had been misunderstood by those standing around the cross as a cry directed to Elijah. They, in turn, gave Him a sour drink and continued to taunt Him. Shortly afterward our Lord uttered these words of committal. He was evidently conscious of the fact that His suffering and sin-bearing had been accomplished. This is what prompted the cry, "Father, into thy hands I commend my spirit" (Luke 23:46).

Analysis of the Prayer

These words were originally spoken by David in the fifth verse of Psalm 31.

The essence of Christ's prayer is in the words *I commend.* The grammar indicates that Jesus is not asking the Father to take His spirit. Christ is herein giving His spirit over to the Father. It is an act of *dedication* rather than petition. The grammar also emphasizes the fact that this was a voluntary action on the part of Jesus. The root idea of the word translated "commend" involves the idea of *trust.* Thus after the almost pathetic cry, "Why hast thou forsaken me?" we have this cry of confident victory. The implication seems to be that the Father answered the unvoiced request hidden in the cry by making Himself known to the Son once more.

Doctrinal Implications of the Prayer

Typical of the other two prayers from the cross, this prayer was offered in a setting of crisis. Like the others, it was deeply emotional. All three prayers from the cross were uttered in the form of loud cries with a sense of extreme earnestness.

Of interest also is the fact that the Father seemed to answer the implied request for help which was stated as a question. This possibly indicates that God answers the cry of the heart even when it is not precisely voiced. I imagine there are many times when I know I need something and in my turmoil I'm really not sure what it is. In semi-confusion I cry out to God. It is comforting to know that He really knows what I need and answers accordingly. This is where the prayer assistance of the indwelling Holy Spirit comes into play (*see* Romans 8:26, 27).

Certainly, if nothing else, the prayers from the cross demonstrate that legitimate prayer can be voiced *any time,* under *any circumstances,* and in *any physical position.*

PART THREE
THE PRAYER TEACHINGS OF JESUS

Jesus taught more fully and definitely on the subject of prayer than on any other single theme. By contrast, a survey of twenty-one leading evangelical seminaries revealed that not one had any required courses directly devoted to the training of future ministers in this vital area.

In my personal experience, I can't recall having ever received one iota of formal classroom instruction on my personal prayer life. They taught me Greek and Hebrew, Church History, and Systematic Theology. They taught me how to organize committees and even tried to teach me song-leading, but no one ever taught me how to pray!

This is tragic. Could it be that the people in the pew don't have effective personal prayer lives because the pulpit is silent on this subject? And could it be that the pulpit is silent because the seminary classroom is correspondingly silent?

So far as the record is concerned, the only time Jesus' disciples ever asked Him to teach them anything was when they came to Him and said, "Lord, teach us to pray . . ." (Luke 11:1). It is this significant body of teaching which will serve as the object of study in the next five chapters.

10
Teachings Concerning Prayer Attitudes

The *proper heart attitude* while praying was of paramount importance to Christ. The study of this aspect of prayer is divided into four parts: (1) privacy; (2) humility; (3) watchfulness; (4) unworthy attitudes.

The Attitude of Privacy: Matthew 6:5,6. Christ preferred privacy in His personal prayer life and He taught His disciples the same principle. He told them, "Thou shalt not be as the hypocrites are . . ." (Matthew 6:5). Prayer in first-century Judaism had been reduced to a system. Among the Pharisees it had become a pious display. Thus Christ referred to them as "hypocrites" or literally, "actors." These "actors" loved to perform their prayers in public places such as street corners and prominent areas in the synagogues in order to impress people with their piety.

Now I want it to be clear that Christ is not at this point condemning public praying. New Testament evidence is available to demonstrate that all of these places can be legitimate places of prayer. Christ Himself prayed publicly on many occasions before vast throngs of people. The real crux of the issue is in the reason for praying: ". . . that they may be seen of men" (verse 5), or to make a display of themselves. It is not the *manner* of prayer but the *motive* of prayer that is being reproved.

In contrast to this hypocritical praying, Christ urged His disciples to pray with a drastically different motive. The words *when thou prayest* indicate that the disciples should make prayer a regular habit. However, the tense of the next word, *enter,* indicates a single act of private prayer. Thus in our regular habit of praying, each single act should be practiced by entering our closet (figuratively speaking).

The entire emphasis is upon *seclusion.* This is evident not only in the idea of going into a closet and shutting the door but also by the repetition of the personal pronoun *thy*. It was "thy closet," "thy door," and "thy Father" (verse 6). All emphasize the concept of isolation.

This isolation not only involves actual physical separation from all distraction, as in a closet, but also emotional seclusion, when physical seclusion is not possible. Even when praying in a public place the believer should be emotionally in the closet talking to the Lord and not to men. The positive value of such secluded praying is the intensely personal filial (child-parent) character of prayer. Prayer in the closet is to thy Father! It is an interchange between persons on an intimate basis.

The Attitude of Humility: Luke 18:9–14. In this extremely scathing parable, the Lord denounces pride in prayer and commends humility. The incidents in the parable are typical of Jewish religious practice in the first century. Actually the parable is not precisely on the subject of prayer, but rather self-confident pride (*see* Luke 18:9). However, the setting certainly makes prayer prominent in the story. Thus in this parable we gain insight into the attitudes of two human beings while they are engaged in prayer; one attitude is acceptable and the other is quite unacceptable.

The parable paints a picture of two men widely different in character and spirit. In fact they are extreme opposites. The first individual is vividly portrayed as the very epitome of pride. He is a Pharisee (*see* verse 10).

In the content of the Pharisee's so-called prayer we can see what a case of full-grown self-righteousness looks like. It is almost nauseating.

In the highest and truest sense, the prayer of this Pharisee was not a prayer at all because he "prayed thus with himself" (verse 11), meaning, "He was praying in favor of himself." This man was conducting his own little "mutual admiration society" in the presence of God and anybody within earshot!

The second prayer (*see* verse 13) is in the sharpest possible contrast to that of the Pharisee. The man praying is identified as a publican. In the New Testament publicans and sinners were commonly coupled together as one class of people. There can be no question that his brief but striking confession, "God be merciful to me a sinner," was a perfectly valid estimate of the man. Actually, the original Greek could be literally translated, *"the* sinner." This individual evidently felt that he was the worst sinner in the whole land! This certainly enhances the emphasis on the man's true humility and repentance. Notice, too, that the Pharisee felt no need and uttered no petition, but the publican felt *only* need and uttered *only* petition.

The major element emphasized is the publican's abject humility and sense of guilt. He is so earnest in his quest and so absorbed in his need before God that he seems completely unconscious of any other person in the temple. He is probably not even aware of the loudmouthed Pharisee standing near the altar. In deep sincerity he just stands there, head down, beating his breast, begging God's mercy.

The climax of the parable indicates that only the prayer voiced in an attitude of sincere, earnest humility produced results. The publican "went down to his house justified," the lesson being, ". . . he that humbleth himself shall be exalted" (verse 14). The word *humbleth* literally means "to make low." The basic idea is that of submission based on love and reverence. A truly humble man will be submissive and this must be the attitude of the man of prayer.

The Attitude of Watchfulness: Mark 14:38; Matthew 26:41. This is not actually a teaching on prayer, but rather a precise *command* from our Lord.

The word *watch* (Mark 14:38) carries the underlying thought of a wakeful frame of mind and keen mental alertness. Thus vigilance is connected to simple praying as a necessary part of achieving desired results. To pray correctly one must be mentally alert and vigilant. Much praying is hampered by a dull, drowsy frame of mind. We get ready for bed at the end of a long day and suddenly remember that we haven't prayed yet, and we begin to mouth over any petitions our fogged mind can conjure up. I don't think such praying gets very far off the ground! This is certainly not biblical praying.

Recently I learned of a woman who was teaching transcendental meditation as a legitimate aspect of Christian prayer. As I understand transcendental meditation, it involves letting the mind go completely blank. If this is true, then there is absolutely no correlation between transcendental meditation and biblical prayer! Actually such a form of meditation could not even be called biblical meditation. Meditation in the Bible involves actively rolling the truths of God's Word around in the mind much as a cow chews its cud! Both meditation and prayer in the Bible necessitate active, sharp, alert mental activity!

The goal of this continuous, sharp, vigilant praying was very practical: ". . . lest ye enter into temptation" (Mark 14:38). The events of that evening certainly proved the truth of Christ's admonition because the disciples did not maintain alert, vigilant prayer, and they did enter into extreme testing. Prayer vigilance is seen as a means of spiritual victory! It is an offensive weapon in the Christian's arsenal. It is a safeguard against defeat.

The Attitudes Considered Unworthy. Jesus not only taught positively what prayer should be but he likewise pointed out colorfully and carefully what it should *not* be! In short, Jesus blasted two improper prayer attitudes. The first was a vengeful spirit, as seen in Luke 9:54,55. When two disciples request a fiery judgment upon certain adversaries (*see* Luke 9:54), Jesus immediately rebuked the *attitude* that prompted such a request: "Ye know not what manner of spirit ye are of" (v. 55). No doubt James and John rationalized that they were influenced by purely religious motives such as hatred of sin or God's honor. Yet in all probability these two Jewish disciples were reflecting wounded pride and/or personal hatred of Samaritans!

An incident that was similar in some respects took place during the trial of Christ. Jesus, surrounded by all of the injustices and false accusations of His captors, could well have prayed for divine judgement to fall upon His adversaries. The text clearly states that He could have called "twelve legions of angels" to His assistance (Matthew 26:53). Yet He did not! Christ did not use prayer as a means of selfish vengeance and neither should we. Such matters as blind zeal, personal resentment, irritated pride, party feelings, violence, and passion can never be legitimate motives for prayer!

The other unworthy attitude which Jesus warned against was the "spirit of sham," which we find in Mark 12:38–40 and Luke 20:45–47. Jesus, in His last public discourse, warned His disciples to beware of the scribes and Pharisees. In these verses it is a specific practice of pharisaical praying that comes under attack. They had the habit of making long prayers. The Lord said it was for a pretense that the long prayers were uttered. The noun translated "for a pretense" (Mark 12:40) actually means "to appear in front." It refers to that which is put forward *to hide the true state of things!* The motive for such long prayers was to put on a pious sham, and by this pretext gain a reputation for piety.

The Pharisees found such a practice helpful in many situations. For example, a Pharisee negotiating a business transaction with a widow might say, "Let's have a time of prayer and commit this whole transaction to the Lord," whereupon he would begin a long and beautiful prayer. The unsuspecting widow would think to herself, "I certainly can trust this individual because no man could pray this way and be a crook." Thus with the widow taken off guard by prayer, the Pharisee would proceed with no difficulty to bilk her! Such a practice brought the most scathing denunciation from our Lord: "These shall receive greater damnation" (Mark 12:40).

Doctrinal Implications Concerning Prayer Attitudes

It becomes apparent that attitude is crucial in effective biblical praying. Nowhere is the axiom "God looketh upon the heart" (*see* 1 Samuel 16:7) more evident than in prayer.

If only one primary attitude were demanded in prayer, there can be little doubt that *sincerity* would receive that designation. Could you ever go into a prayer closet and address our all-knowing God with dishonesty and insincerity? Sincerity and honesty are the order of the day in our prayer lives.

Certainly *humility* would also rank high on the list of important prayer attitudes and humility involves submissiveness by its very definition. The publican, in utter submissiveness, thrust himself totally upon God's mercy. A humble, submissive heart is a *dependent* heart, and dependence is the very core of biblical prayer.

Humble submission also begets *unselfishness*. Show me a man who is willing to submit and not insist upon his own right, and I will show you an unselfish individual. Why do you want a better job? Why do you want to be a better teacher? If it's simply to selfishly stimulate your ego, you may be praying unbiblically.

By way of conclusion, let it be said that prayer, as represented in these teachings, must spring from an emotional involvement. *Indifferent, ritualistic praying cannot be legitimately gathered from any of these lessons.* A man who knows he's in spiritual danger does not recite liturgy without emotion! I cannot imagine the publican reading a prewritten prayer in a monotone while flaying away at his breast. I cannot conceive of any of my children entering privately into a room with me and then simply reciting beautiful words in an emotionless, rote fashion. Frankly, I would be deeply hurt to think that they realized I was in the room with them and then conducted themselves in such a way. I wonder what the Father thinks when His children do such things and call it prayer?

11
Teachings Concerning Persistence

No phase of prayer is more emphasized in the Gospels than persistence. Successful praying often involves relentless, persistent asking over a long period of time. Jesus' teaching on this subject centers mainly around two parables: the friend at midnight (Luke 11:5–8) and the unjust judge (Luke 18:1–8). Because these two stories are parables and not allegories, it should be kept in mind that they each teach one main truth. This does not completely rule out other legitimate applications, but it does mean that one basic concept is intended.

The Parable of the Friend at Midnight: Luke 11:5–13. Jesus had been praying in a certain place, and His disciples suddenly came upon Him. The sight of a man praying was not unusual in first-century Palestine, but this was something different. By this time the disciples had come to realize that Jesus' praying was a *force* rather than a *form* and they desired to know the secret. Our Lord gave this parable to teach them the manner in which prayer petitions are to be voiced.

Analysis of the Parable: Luke 11:5–8. The situation which prompted the man to go next door and make a rather bold request of his neighbor was a *crisis!* In that culture at that time, it was a terrible disgrace not to offer a guest in your home some refreshment. The man went to his cupboard and, like Old Mother Hubbard's, it was bare. The host had "nothing to set before" his guest (Luke 11:6). This man was in trouble. I know it sounds silly by our set of values, but in that culture it was a serious thing. A few years ago I was in Lebanon and our Arab guide challenged us to walk up to any house in that village, knock on the door, and see if the people inside wouldn't offer us some refreshment before we left. He said this was still a very real thing to the people in that part of the world.

This man in the parable was in a terribly embarrassing position. So he did something he would normally never have dreamed of doing.

Even though it was midnight he marched to his neighbor's house and began to pound on the door. The point our Lord wants us to see is that *the man's petition was born out of a crisis which prompted a genuine sense of need!* The person to whom the man went for assistance was a friend who did comply, but only after much persistence. The implication is obvious. If a mere friend could be moved by persistent asking, surely much more could be expected from a Father.

Note also the manner in which this desperate man petitioned his friend—he went to him *directly.* The fellow didn't try to get anyone to intercede for him. In the application of this parable, our Lord clearly shows that we can go straight to the Father with our desires. The man did not deluge his friend with words but spoke frankly and pointedly. He told the friend exactly what he wanted: "Lend me three loaves" (verse 5). He didn't say, "Give me some groceries," or "Give me food!" He specified the nature of the refreshment and the amount desired. The major truth our Lord was trying to teach by this parable was "importunity." Clearly the request was granted "because of his importunity" (verse 8). Virtually all agree that this clause is the crux of the parable. Normal friendship would never have gotten the request granted that night. It was simply too inconvenient. It took more than asking. It took importunate asking!

But what precisely does "importunate" mean? Two ideas are present in the word. First and basic is the concept of *shamelessness.* Was it not a shameless act to pound on the neighbor's door at midnight? It was shameless to the point of effrontery, but a fellow really in trouble will not hesitate to be shameless and bold! He needed something drastically and, therefore, had an overwhelming desire to get it! That's what importunate asking involves. However, importunity involves more. It also involves *persistence!* The fellow simply wouldn't give up! He just kept pounding on the door asking for bread! If a man is in enough trouble he will not only be shameless but persistent as well. Thus importunate asking involves dogged, tenacious persistence reaching the point of shamelessness! This is the way Jesus taught us to bring our petitions to the Father!

Analysis of the Explanation of the Parable: Luke 11:9–13. In addition to the parable on prayer, Jesus now adds His own specific commands regarding dogged persistence (*see* verses 9, 10). The words *ask, seek,* and *knock* are all in a verb tense that emphasizes continuous action. They could be literally translated, "Keep on asking, keep on seeking, keep on knocking." Seeking is a more intense expression than asking, and knocking is more intense than either asking or seeking. In fact, the word translated "knock" is the picture of a man beating on a door with vigorous blows! The three taken together build up to a real climax of persistent fervor. Prayer is herein set in graphic terms of earnest, sincere, almost desperate asking! This is hardly the picture that comes to mind when most of us sing the familiar hymn "Sweet Hour of Prayer." Prayer as pictured in this lesson is work—hard work!

To that person who does persist, the Lord gives the encouraging promise: "For every one that asketh receiveth; and he that seeketh findeth; and to him that knocketh it shall be opened" (Luke 11:10). The reason for tough, persistent prayer is that it will get results—not just some of the time, but all of the time!

Clearly the argument of verses 11–13 is from the lesser to the greater: from what faulty fathers do to what the perfect Father in heaven does. In each case the object asked for by the child is similar in appearance to the object suggested as a substitute. The point is that of deception. An earthly father would not give his son a stone, a snake, or a scorpion! It is inconceivable to imagine a little fellow asking his dad for a fish, and his father trying to pass a snake off on him! Every now and then we read of some horrible person who deceives a small child into thinking he's getting a piece of candy, when it is really poison. Yet even in our sick society, it would be considered unthinkable for a *father* to do that to his own kids! The point, then, is obvious: If earthly dads, with all their faults, will give good things to their children, how much more can we depend upon our perfect heavenly Father to answer the fervent, persistent petitions of His children in the best possible manner.

Thus Christ's lesson on prayer was one long discussion on *petition!* Not one word is taught about how to thank God, praise God, or adore God! This is not a lesson on how to have effective conversation with God, but on how to effectively ask Him for things! In the strongest possible manner, Jesus taught that the crux of prayer was *petition—explicit petition—urgent petition—persistent petition!* To be sure, this is quite a different emphasis than is to be found in virtually all published works on the subject of prayer.

Analysis of the Parable of the Unjust Judge: Luke 18:1–8. The basic thrust of this parable is to show that though the heavens appear to be silent and prayers seem to fall on deaf ears, God, much more surely than the unjust judge, will respond to persistent prayer. It teaches us to always pray in spite of the temptation to give up when the answer is delayed! The parable is centered around two characters, a certain judge and a needy widow. The story was drawn directly from the cultural situation of that day, and must have caused immediate attention. The chief feature our Lord wished to convey concerning the judge in the story was the fact that he "feared not God, neither regarded man" (Luke 18:2). The unfavorable character of the judge is obviously intended to point up the impossibility of anyone ever receiving any consideration from such a person.

The second character in the parable is described simply as "a widow." In that culture no other descriptive words were necessary because "a widow" conveyed the idea of helplessness all by itself. A helpless widow would be the most unlikely person to persuade this unscrupulous judge.

The widow possessed only one weapon, which she used most effectively. That weapon was dogged, relentless *persistence!* The verb tense of the words "she came" used to describe the widow's action indicates not a single act but repeated, continual acts of coming (*see* Luke 18:3). The whole picture is made even more graphic by the usage of the same verb tense for the judge's response. (v. 4). Do you get the picture? The widow kept persistently coming and the old judge kept tenaciously refusing, day after day! It reached the point where the judge almost hated to go to the office in the morning! He began dreaming of that bothersome woman at night. Yet his pride could not let him give in to her relentless petitioning. This contest may have gone on for weeks!

Finally the judge, like all mortal men, began to wear down under such gentle but relentless pressure. He began to rationalize. The phrase "Though I fear not God, nor regard man" (verse 4) lets us know that the essential character of the judge hadn't changed one bit. His change in action regarding the widow's request was clearly not due to a change in character. It wasn't because he had gone to a revival meeting and received a conversion experience.

The judge's attitude change was solely due to the woman's dogged tenacity and nothing else (*see* v. 5). In effect, the judge finally threw up his hands and said, "This woman keeps coming around here day after day and it's driving me out of my mind! Just to get her off my back I'm going to grant her request." And why did Jesus tell this story? "That men ought always to pray, and not to faint" (verse 1).

Analysis of the Parable's Application: Luke 18:6–8. Having illustrated the effective nature of persistent prayer, the Lord brings out what He considers the significant implication drawn from the judge's remarks. In verse 7 Jesus emphasizes the words: 'And . . . God. . . ."' Grammatically this could be legitimately translated "But . . . God," to show that there is a basic contrast between the judge and God. This is important in the understanding of the parable. All that the judge was, God is not, and conversely all that God is, the judge was not. The judge had no care for God or man, but our God cares! The corrupt judge was indifferent for a time to the plea of the woman; when he finally did give in, it was solely for selfish reasons. God is never indifferent and never grants requests for selfish reasons. Thus an indifferent and unjust judge is placed over against the just and gracious God. It is selfishness contrasted to holiness. It is unwillingness contrasted to eagerness.

Yet in spite of the fact that God and the judge are emphatically contrasted, there is one point where God and the judge are not in contrast. That is the fact of delay! God, like the judge, does at times delay His response to the petitions of His children as seen by the words "though he bear long with them" (v. 7). However, when God delays, it's because He knows that the time is not right; He genuinely desires to develop His children through the experience of the delay. God's delays are part of the "all things" that He is using to work together to accomplish His good purpose in our lives (Romans 8:28). During the delay we, like the widow, are to "cry day and night unto him . . ." (Luke 18:7) with persistent pleadings. Christ categorically assures us that God will indeed respond to persistent prayers of "his own elect" (v. 7).

Conclusion

Christ would have us realize this: *Persistent prayer will pay off.* These parables are practical guides for believers during the entire time of our Lord's absence. As this age gets increasingly more difficult, as the Lord's coming grows even closer, we can expect things to get worse. The only way a child of God can survive under such adverse conditions is to "hang in there" with tough, persistent praying.

Perseverance in prayer is neither to wear God down nor to cause Him to grant a request in exasperation. The contrasts emphasized in these two parables clearly bears this out. Jesus never once hints that persistence can make God more willing to answer prayer. God is pictured as always willing to aid His children when they call upon Him.

Thus, while the reality of persistence cannot be denied in Scripture, its precise function remains a problem. Why does a gracious, loving God want us to keep asking day after day until the answer comes? Why not ask only once and sit back in faith and wait for the answer? If you will permit, I would like to reserve a discussion of these matters until the final section of this book. By that time we will have had an opportunity to investigate all the evidence in the Gospels that has a bearing on the subject.

12
Teachings Concerning Content

Most of what we learn of the content of prayer is derived from a study of the personal prayers of Jesus. Without doubt the greatest insights gained from Christ's direct teachings are the six petitions contained in the model prayer commonly referred to as the Lord's Prayer (*see* Matthew 6:9–13 and Luke 11:1–4). Because I have already analyzed this prayer quite thoroughly in an earlier chapter, no extensive study of it will be repeated at this point.

By way of the briefest review, it was seen that Christ instructed that requests be offered for the following things: (1) the sanctity of the Father's name; (2) the coming of God's kingdom soon; (3) the accomplishment of God's purposes on this earth; (4) the supply of needed material items; (5) the forgiveness of personal sins; (6) protection from evil.

The rest of Christ's direct teachings on prayer content would add only two items to the six specified above: (1) Christ instructed prayer for persecutors and (2) He specifically instructed prayer for laborers.

Prayer for Persecutors: Matthew 5:44; Luke 6:27, 28. So far as the record is concerned, the only time Jesus ever *specifically* gave instruction concerning prayer for a non-Christian was in Matthew 5:44 and its parallel in Luke 6:27, 28. Both passages are found in the context of the Sermon on the Mount. Thus prayer for persecutors was the first lesson on prayer given by Jesus.

In both Matthew and Luke the passage begins with an emphatic "I say" that reveals authoritative instruction. First the command is to "love your enemies" (Matthew 5:44) which in itself was startling and new to the first-century Jewish mind. But then Christ continues by commanding positive prayer for those enemies who were actually persecuting them. The actual command, "Pray for them," carries the idea of praying for them continuously. Christ is not saying to pray for your persecutors once but to keep on praying for them even as they continue to torment you. Do you have a boss who's mistreating you? What should you do about it? Fight back? Try and get back at him in some way? No! Keep on praying for him! Wow! That's a different approach, to say the least. Certainly only true love, which Jesus puts in the believer's heart, could possibly produce this kind of praying.

Matthew designates the objects of prayer as people who "despitefully use and persecute" the believer (*see* Matthew 5:44). The word translated "despitefully use" carries the idea of insulting and general harassment of an individual. The word *persecute* is somewhat more restricted. Some contend it has special reference to religious persecutors. If this is true, it can be shown historically that religious persecutors are generally folk who are most difficult to deal with.

We are not specifically told what type of requests are to be voiced to the Father on behalf of our enemies. The word *pray* is a word meaning simply praying to God in a general sense. The only possible hint must be inferred from the prepositions. Luke leaves the issue somewhat vague because the word *for* in the phrase "pray for them . . ." (Luke 6:28) has the basic meaning of "concerning" or "about." Thus the believer is simply commanded to pray *concerning* his enemy.

Matthew is quite a bit more precise, however. He uses a different Greek preposition that carries the root idea "in behalf of," which can mean "for the benefit of" in this instance. Thus the passage seems to teach that the prayer is to be *for the benefit of* the persecutor in some manner. Now certainly the greatest possible benefit for an enemy would be his salvation. So by implication it would seem to be permissible to pray for God to save the souls of sinful men.

The purpose for this type of conduct toward our enemies is stated in Matthew 5:45: "That ye may be the children of your Father which is in heaven." This statement must not be taken to mean that such actions cause us to become children of God. This would be a salvation of works, which the New Testament opposes (*see* Ephesians 2:8, 9). The expression "that ye may be" refers to the *establishing* of a fact. Such loving, prayerful action toward enemies does not make a man a Christian but it furnishes open, concrete evidence that he really is a child of God. It gives evidence of sonship. It does not create sonship.

Prayer for Laborers: Matthew 9:38; Luke 10:1, 2. This command was given in view of Christ's compassion for the pathetic and lost condition of the masses of people mentioned in Matthew 9:36. But the specific reason is evidently the labor shortage mentioned in verse 37.

The word translated "pray" emphasizes the idea of making an urgent request or beseeching. Thus it indicates the idea of petition but places great emphasis on the idea of expressing need.

The purpose of such praying is stated in the phrase "that he will send forth labourers . . ." (Matthew 9:38). The Lord does not tell us the exact words to pray but we are told to pray for the purpose of gaining an increase in the Lord's labor force. The words *send forth* (verse 38) are from a very strong Greek word meaning, "to thrust out, drive out, or push out." The word conveys the idea of being thrust out, even by violent means if necessary. Putting all this together, the believer is herein instructed to urgently pray to God that laborers may decisively be pushed out (violently if necessary) into the needy harvest fields of this world!

It clearly seems to teach a tie-in between prayer and the supplying of missionary personnel, both professional and nonprofessional. Someone might object by saying, "God will most certainly bring in His harvest of souls," or "Why ask God for the success of His own work?" Yet even a brief survey of prayer as taught and practiced by Jesus will reveal numerous instances of similar petitions. Take, for example, the second petition of the Lord's Prayer: "Thy will be done in earth, as it is in heaven" (Matthew 6:10). The same logic that says, "Why pray because God is sovereign?" could just as well say, "Why preach? God is sovereign and can save sinners without using men to herald the message." However, the facts of both history and Scripture tell us that God does use both the witness of men and the prayers of men in accomplishing His program. The entire matter goes beyond the limits of human understanding. Indeed, we are clearly told that God's ways are "past finding out" (Romans 11:33). Do you need workers in your Sunday school? Is there a drastic shortage of foreign missionary personnel? God says pray! So often we engage in fancy recruitment programs and exert tremendous energy; yet when all the dust settles, the labor shortage still persists. Why? Because we haven't utilized God's method in coping with the problem!

Now once a Christian really gets concerned and starts earnestly praying for God to do something about the desperate need for more laborers in the overripe harvest fields of the world, something else will happen! Often that Christian will find himself being thrust forth into the harvest! There is many a missionary on a foreign field today who will tell you that his interest in missions started with a genuine concern for the lost which motivated fervent prayer for laborers. This truth seems to be implied in this very passage under consideration. Christ commands the twelve Apostles to pray for God to thrust forth laborers (*see* Matthew 9:38), and then immediately sends those same Apostles forth on a missionary endeavor (*see* Matthew 10:1–7). The same thing happened on another occasion when Jesus urged seventy select disciples to pray for God to provide workers, and then He sent them out as workers (*see* Luke 10:1, 2). When hearts are willing to pray for a certain undertaking, they are often likewise ready to assist in having it carried out.

The subjective effect upon the person doing the praying is self-evident. However, we must never conclude that this is the only reason our Lord commanded us to pray in this fashion. The strong command to urgently beseech the Father indicates that such petitions are more than just a clever plan by God to make the person praying willing to be a worker himself. In some manner, earnest petition is necessary in the outworking of God's plan.

Amazingly, the Lord did not instruct prayer for the *harvest* but for the *harvesters!* Here was an obvious evangelistic need. The harvest was plenteous (*see* Matthew 9:37), but instead of instructing the disciples to pray for the salvation of lost souls, He said to pray for the thrusting forth of laborers. In twenty years in the ministry associating freely with prayer groups from every level of Christian society, I think I can safely state that there are probably ten petitions uttered for the salvation of lost sinners (the harvest) for every one uttered for the thrusting forth of laborers into the harvest. Yet Christ explicitly and definitely taught the latter but never explicitly and definitely taught the former. Does this not indicate how far afield the emphasis of our current prayer practice is from the teachings of the New Testament?

Doctrinal Implications of Prayer Content

The Lord specifically taught that we should pray for the Father to send forth laborers into the harvest of unsaved men. The Lord also taught persistent prayer for the benefit of those who might persecute a believer. By implication this could involve prayer for the salvation of the persecutor.

Christ likewise taught that petitions should include the immediate needs of the believer. By implication every conceivable personal need is legitimate, both spiritual and material. Yet the spiritual needs unquestionably dominate our Lord's teachings. Only the teaching concerning daily bread gives direct legitimacy for petitions for material things.

Again, prayer as seen in Christ's lessons on content is clearly petitionary in nature. In all these lessons, not one word is given to teach thanksgiving, adoration, or praise. When Christ taught about the content of prayer it always pertained to the types of petitions to bring before the Father. The petitions were always pictured as arising from a sense of need—a need resulting from a crisis situation. When you pray for a fellow who's persecuting you, there is a need and a crisis involved in that situation! Because of a crisis context, earnestness in petition is once more obvious; the inevitable accompaniment of earnest petitions will be specific petitions. This aspect of being specific in prayer is quite obvious in the lesson on laborers but it corresponds to our Lord's personal practice of prayer, as we have already observed.

The most unusual aspect of all of Jesus' teachings on prayer content is the total lack of explicit, specific prayer instruction pertaining to the salvation of lost men and women. But certainly it cannot be said by any serious student of Jesus' life and teachings that He lacked concern for the unregenerate masses. He insisted that He had come to lead sinners to repentance. He wept over Jerusalem. He grieved over the multitudes. The very thing that prompted His command to pray for the thrusting forth of laborers was the fact that He saw the multitudes and "was moved with compassion on them . . ." (Matthew 9:36). No, the lack of a specific command to pray for the salvation of the lost cannot be attributed to a lack of concern on the part of Christ. Could it be that the key to successful evangelistic praying is not so much prayer for the specific salvation of individual men as prayer for God to burden the heart of Christian people to see the need of the whitened harvest fields and get themselves in a position spiritually where God can thrust them forth as active, aggressive reapers?

In Dr. Lewis Chafer's very excellent work *True Evangelism,* prayer is correctly assigned as the key ingredient in effective evangelism. He tells us that if we would do more talking to God about men, we would not need to talk to men so much about God. With this I heartily agree! But what Dr. Chafer has in mind when he speaks of "talking with God about men" is that we Christians should pray for the salvation of lost men. However, would it not be more in keeping with the emphasis of Jesus to make the burden of our evangelistic praying prayer for the *laborers* rather than the *harvest* (unsaved men)? By this I mean we should petition God vigorously to burden the hearts of Christians concerning the harvest.

13
Teachings Concerning Prayer Conditions
(Part One)

An important consideration in any discussion of prayer is the matter of conditions. If prayer is basically asking God for things, what, if any, are the qualifying conditions which must be met if a person's requests are to be granted? Some of the prayer promises of Christ have seemed on the surface to be unconditional in nature; at least no condition is directly stated in the promises themselves. The two outstanding examples are Matthew 7:7, 8 and Luke 11:9, 10. In discussing these verses earlier in this book, it was discovered that implicit conditions were to be found in the immediate context. The fact is that there is no such thing in the New Testament as *unconditional prayer.* All biblical prayer promises are either conditioned *explicitly* or *implicitly.*

In His teachings, Christ explicitly taught three major conditions for individual prayer: (1) faith; (2) abiding; (3) prayer in His name. In Christ's own prayer life, another condition becomes very evident. Christ always prayed in accordance with *the will of the Father.* Strangely, however, the will of God was never actually given as a condition for prayer in our Lord's teachings. Yet a consideration of the three definite conditions stated above will reveal that when rightly understood, they all necessitate a believer praying in God's will. Therefore, the will of God seems to be the underlying condition for successful praying. It is the man whose heart supremely yearns for God's glory and the accomplishment of His will who prays meaningfully.

One more item needs mentioning before we begin an analysis of the various conditions. Many feel that Christ actually gave one more prayer condition: "That if two of you shall agree on earth as touching any thing that they shall ask, it shall be done for them of my Father

which is in heaven" (Matthew 18:19). However, a careful consideration of the context will reveal that Christ gave this promise in connection with a discussion of discipline within a local church. Actually
Matthew 18:15–20 constitutes a unit of thought and it is quite unfair
to isolate verse 19 and interpret it independently. If a person handles
the statement in its setting, the verse is part of Christ's instructions
to a local church as to how to excommunicate an erring member if
that should ever be necessary. Verse 19 does not constitute a prayer
promise to individual Christians *directly.*

Faith as a Condition

The direct instructions of Christ concerning faith in relation to
prayer center around two instances: (1) the powerless disciples (*see*
Matthew 17:20, 21 and Mark 9:23–29) and (2) the parable of the
withered fig tree (*see* Matthew 21:17–22 and Mark 11:20–24). In both
instances, the teachings stemmed from everyday life experiences and
thus their practicality becomes self-evident.

The Powerless Disciples: Matthew 17:20, 21; Mark 9:23–29. A dis-
traught father had brought his demon-possessed son to the disciples
for healing, but they failed utterly to help the boy. When Christ
arrived, the father told Him of the disciples' inability to help, and
requested that He aid the lad (*see* Matthew 17:14–16). At the Lord's
command, the demon immediately departed (*see* Matthew 17:18).
Christ also rebuked the assembled crowd in strong and severe language for their faithlessness (*see* Matthew 17:17). Naturally the disciples were included in Christ's bitter denunciation. Their failure was
due to "unbelief" which literally means, "little faith." The disciples
simply had too little faith for the occasion. Evidently it does not
necessarily need to be great faith because He said it can be "as a grain
of mustard seed" (Matthew 17:20) but it must be a *consistent* faith.
The mustard seed was tiny but had an amazing ability to shoot up into
a flowering plant. Thus even a little faith in God when consistently
applied can, at a critical moment, shoot up into a mighty power and
accomplish wonders. This type of faith can be seen operating in the
life of Gideon and many other great men of the Scriptures.

Correct prayer is impossible apart from faith (*see* James 1:6). Thus it is prayer conditioned upon faith that exercises mountain-removing power. A deficiency in faith renders prayer ineffective. The nine disciples had attempted to cast out the demon without relying upon God's power which is available through prayer. Unbelief and prayerlessness are often companions and are sure to result in spiritual impotence!

The phrase "and fasting" (Mark 9:29) was omitted in many of the earliest and best Greek manuscripts, and was probably not part of the original text of Scripture. After all, there would have been no opportunity for the disciples to have fasted in this situation, but they surely could have trusted and prayed. The language makes it clear that had this been done, the power of God would have been released and the demon would have been cast out.

The Withered Fig Tree: Mark 11:20–24; Matthew 21:17–22. The thought here is that the Christian must continually believe that what he is asking for is happening right then! Faith is to be exercised *continuously* which, in the very nature of the case, would imply a note of expectation. When you believe something is really going to happen, you then expect it to happen. This is the kind of consistent faith herein advocated by our Lord. It is this faith which is the basis of prayer.

Jesus no doubt uses an exaggerated expression when He declares that faith can remove mountains (*see* Mark 11:23), but the fact remains that while God will not grant everything that might be mentioned, nevertheless He is able to remove mountains (literally or figuratively) if the need arises and He so wills.

The Lord then generalizes from a mountain to "What things soever ye desire" (verse 24). The word *desire* could be better translated "ask." The word *and* separating the two verbs *ask* and *pray* indicates that they both refer to the *same action. Praying, then, is asking, and asking God for things is praying!* This obviously brings the petitionary nature of prayer into prominence.

All of this continuous and/or repeated petitionary praying is to be done in an *attitude of faith.* In fact, the idea of continuous faith is emphasized by the word *receive* (*see* verse 24). Grammatically the action of the verb *receive* actually takes place before the action described in the verb *believe.* The whole clause could be translated, "Go on believing that you have received it." The fulfillment is seen before it happens! This dramatically emphasizes the aspect of expectancy in faith. Prayer requests are to be characterized by an unshakeable confidence that they will be granted. We are to go on believing even while asking, knowing that God has already heard and answered our petition!

The certainty of an answer to prayer offered with this kind of expectant faith is evident in the phrase ". . . ye shall have them" (verse 24). The passage leaves no doubt that God will most certainly answer this kind of praying—not some of the time, but all of the time!

Doctrinal Implications of Prayer-Faith

The fact that faith is a condition for successful praying cannot be denied. Faith guarantees to the one exercising it the answer to his prayer, even though that answer may be delayed and the thing asked for is not in his possession. Faith is capable of releasing tremendous divine power. In fact Jesus seems to attribute a sort of omnipotence (all power) to faith: ". . . and nothing shall be impossible unto you" (Matthew 17:20). Evidently even a very small amount of genuine faith has tremendous potential. Though the faith need not be great in *quantity,* it must be of the proper *quality* to be effective. It must be constant and unwavering. It is never pictured as intermittent bursts of confidence but always as a quiet, steady, growing trust. Such quiet, confident faith will ask boldly and fervently with an actual expectation that God is really hearing and will actually answer in His own way and in His own time. A man with this kind of prayer-faith will inevitably carry his umbrella when He asks God to send rain!

Probably the major difference of opinion with regard to prayer-faith centers around the question concerning the *object* of that faith. If faith consists of placing confidence in someone or something, what precisely is that person or thing? Two divergent opinions on this issue will be found in most general prayer literature:

(1) Prayer-faith is an unswerving confidence applied to the petition itself. It is complete assurance that the *thing requested* will be granted.

(2) Prayer-faith is an absolute confidence applied to the *source* of the request. It is complete reliance upon the one toward whom you are looking to grant the request. Thus, like saving faith, it is a committal to God without reservation.

The first position would contend that if a person believed consistently and strongly enough that a mountain would be removed, it would be removed. It's all a question of whether or not you believe strongly enough that it is going to happen! Thus faith becomes sort of a magical force in and of itself. The error in such thinking lies not so much in an overemphasis upon faith as in a misunderstanding of the true nature of biblical faith.

A study of the word *faith* in the Gospels will reveal that its ultimate object is always a *person* and not a *thing.* Every occurrence, so far as I can determine, will either state or imply a person in whom ultimate confidence is placed. Most certainly this is the teaching of the passage (*see* Mark 11:23, 24) we have just considered.

In answer to Peter's question regarding the withered fig tree, Jesus' first remark was, "Have faith in God" (Mark 11:22). Following this, the Lord proceeded to expound upon faith as a prayer condition. Clearly, then, Jesus sought to turn the thought of the disciples to faith as a matter of *dependence on God* before discussing the possibilities of exercising such faith. Thus it is not *faith in faith* or *faith in your request* but *faith in God* that is an effectual condition to successful praying.

It is actually impossible to exercise faith in a prayer-petition without at the same time having faith in God, from whom the answer must come. Faith that a thing shall be given implies faith in the person from whom we expect it. You cannot believe in a man's promise until you first believe in the man himself! Suppose I promise you ten dollars if you meet me in the front of the auditorium when class is over. If you really think about it, you couldn't believe my promise without having confidence in me as a person.

Prayer-faith, then, is not an abstract "something" which Christians must exert in order for God to grant their requests. *Faith is a trusting confidence in the total Person of God.* Notice, if you will, that I said the *total* Person of God. This involves not only God's ability but also

His knowledge and love. It is not just a confidence as to whether or not God is able to remove the mountain but it is also a confidence that God *knows* if it is really best for the mountain to be removed, and in what direction it should be moved. Prayer-faith says, "Father, from my limited perspective it looks as if it is best for the mountain to be removed, and I'm asking You to remove it. Now, Father, there is no doubt whatsoever in my mind that You are fully capable of removing this mountain; but I also have confidence in Your love and wisdom as to whether or not it really should be removed."

Actually, once faith is rightly understood, prayer without faith is self-contradictory. It is like asking a man for something and at the same time having no confidence at all that he will grant your request. Viewed in this fashion, faith becomes an aspect of *submission to God's will.* I say this because the person who is completely dependent on God is, of necessity, submissive to that God. By way of illustration, a man who is sitting in a chair is both *totally* dependent upon the chair to keep him a foot and a half off the floor, and *completely* submissive to the chair at one and the same time. Thus in exercising faith in the chair he must in a real sense submit to the chair. So a man really praying in dependence upon God (faith) will at the same time be in submission to that God.

On this basis it is not the *amount* of the faith but the *object* of faith that is significant. This kind of faith in a quantity as insignificant as a grain of mustard seed can produce tremendous results. It is the *fact* of the Christian's faith in God, not the strength of that faith, which is emphasized in Christ's lessons on prayer.

Abiding as a Condition

Another element upon which Christ conditioned successful praying was that of "abiding." Though implied elsewhere, it is explicitly stated only in John 15:7. This prayer condition is found in the midst of a crucial discourse the Lord gave His disciples in the final hours of His earthly ministry. Many men who normally see little or no direct relevance for Jesus' earthly teachings to the New Testament Church, freely acknowledge this discourse as being directly applicable to this age.

Definition of the Term Abide

Of supreme importance to a proper exegesis of the prayer condition found in John 15:7 is a clear understanding of the term *abide*. Even a casual survey of the commentaries will reveal a lack of sharp, precise definition with respect to this term. Therefore, it is deemed wise to undertake a brief word study prior to our actual analysis of the entire passage.

The word *abide* is found in the New Testament predominately in the writings of the Apostle John. It is used ninety-three times in the New Testament, and sixty-three of those are in John's writings. *Abide* carries the basic meaning "to remain." In the passage we are considering, the word *abide* is always followed by the preposition *in,* so the total concept is "abide in." The idea is to remain in vital contact with someone or something. In John's writings the "abide in" construction is used to depict the spiritual relationship existing between Christ and the Father, and between Christ and the believer. Used in this manner, the "abide in" idea depicts one person wholly joined with, totally submissive to, and dependent upon another. It involves being under the power and influence of another. It seems to me that to abide in Christ is simply to be sold out to Christ and His cause. It's quite similar to the truth Paul presents in Romans 12:1 when he says, ". . . present your bodies a living sacrifice, holy, acceptable unto God, which is your reasonable service." A person so committed would be abiding in Christ.

Analysis of Abiding as a Condition

The prayer teaching relative to abiding is found in connection with Christ's discussion of the True Vine, wherein the relationship between Christ and the believer is set forth as a branch united to a vine (Christ). The primary thrust of the analogy is spiritual productivity. Christ used this figure to teach disciples how they can be fruitful, growing Christians (*see* John 15:1–8).

The admonition is stated in the form of a condition: "If ye abide in me . . ." (verse 7). The grammar indicates that the Lord fully expected the disciples to meet the condition and become fruitful Christians by abiding in Him. The second clause, ". . . and my words abide in you . . ." (verse 7), is a further explanation of what it really means to abide in Christ. The Lord further clarifies the "abiding" concept in verse 10: "If ye keep my commandments, ye shall abide in my love. . . ."

It is my honest opinion that all three aspects—abiding in Christ's person, having Christ's words abiding in the believer, and abiding in the love of Christ, are but various aspects of the same essential reality. Together they constitute the significance of Christ's command, "Abide in me . . ." (verse 4).

To abide in Christ, then, is to be so adjusted to Christ as to have uninterrupted fellowship with Him. It is remaining in reliance upon Him, of being open to receive from Him the spiritual vitality for successful fruit bearing. A believer is abiding when he decides to consciously depend upon Jesus Christ as the *condition* for being a fruitful Christian. Beyond question, the classic example of this type of abiding is to be found in the earthly life of our Lord. He constantly remained in conscious harmony with the Father.

The second phase of this prayer condition concerns "My words abiding in you" (*see* verse 7). Notice the slight shift from a similar statement in verse 4: "Abide in me, and I in you." This time instead of saying, "I in you," our Lord said, ". . . my words abide in you. . . ." The change in the second clause in verse 7 indicates that Jesus wished to point out that it is the *remembrance of* and *meditation upon* His words which is the earmark of the disciple who is truly abiding in Christ.

The expression translated "words" could also just as well be translated "sayings." The idea involved refers to the principles of truth and life which Christ had communicated to the disciples. It becomes increasingly apparent that abiding in Christ's sayings involves more than simply reading or being exposed to them. It involves submission to them and living in accordance with them. Jesus used the same Greek word that is translated "abide" in John 8:31, when He urged believers to "continue in my word." Consequently, the concept of *knowing* and *obeying* Christ's words is involved in this prayer condition. To put it very simply, abiding in Christ is, in reality, practicing the words of the old hymn "Trust and Obey": "Trust and obey, for there's no other way/To be happy in Jesus,/But to trust and obey." For those believers who meet the condition of abiding, the promise is certain: "Ye shall ask what ye will, and it shall be done unto you" (John 15:7).

Doctrinal Implications of Abiding

Abiding as a prayer condition involves the perpetuation of a close, communal relationship between Christ and the believer. No matter what effort is made to explain, it remains a somewhat mystical relationship. Instruction can proceed just so far and ultimately it must be *caught* rather than *taught*. It must be lived and experienced rather than explained.

However, an obvious implication of abiding is *submission* to Christ and His words. It would be impossible for a believer to be abiding in Christ and be in a state of self-willed rebellion against Jesus Christ and His teachings. A carnal Christian is not an abiding Christian and, therefore, cannot lay claim to the prayer promises of Jesus. The Father, in His grace, may answer the prayer of a willful Christian, but He is not obligated to do so!

Thus it is apparent that abiding is directly related to the will of God. A perfect relationship of abiding would assure complete harmony with God's will. Thus, as was true in our previous discussion of faith, the condition of abiding is simply another way of saying, ". . . not my will, but thine, be done" (Luke 22:42).

14
Teachings Concerning Prayer Conditions (Part Two)

A third significant condition for successful praying was to "ask in my name" (John 14:13). No less than six times, Jesus urged the disciples to pray in this fashion. These six statements are found in four separate passages in the Upper Room Discourse (*see* John 13–16). If Jesus Christ repeated something to those disciples six times that night, it must have been pretty important!

Analysis of John 14:12–14; 15:16; 16:23–24. In John 14:10, 11, Jesus claimed to be the Father's perfect representative through whom the Father's own work was to be accomplished. He proceeded to insist that those who are true disciples will also do the Father's work in an even greater measure (*see* John 14:12). Then, as if coming to the heart of His message, the Lord indicated *how* these greater works would be accomplished: ". . . because I go unto my Father. And whatsoever ye shall ask in my name, that will I do . . ." (John 14:12,13). The word *because* of verse 12 governs the next two clauses: "I go unto my Father" and "whatsoever ye shall ask in my name."

Thus Christ gave two reasons that the believer would be able to do greater works. The first reason was "I go unto my Father." At first glance His going away might seem totally unrelated to the matter of the believer's performing greater works. However, a little later in this same discourse Christ explained the connection: "It is expedient for you that I go away: for if I go not away, the Comforter will not come unto you; but if I depart, I will send him unto you" (John 16:7). Do you see the connection now? His going away would mean the coming of the Holy Spirit to indwell and empower the disciples.

The second reason believers will be able to accomplish greater works is, "Whatsoever ye shall ask in my name, that will I do . . ." (John 14:13). Thus prayer in Christ's name is a means by which the disciple will be able to do greater works. Hence prayer is directly associated with the *accomplishment of activity!* This kind of prayer will accomplish things.

The promise to grant "whatsoever" the disciple might request is conditioned by the phrase "shall ask in my name." Clearly Christ did not promise that all prayer would be answered—only prayer that is offered "in my name." The conditional clause, however, is stated in a way that indicates by its grammar that Christ fully expected the disciples in the future to take Him up on His offer and actually ask for things in His name. For those who do ask in this manner, there is the unquestionable guarantee "that will I do." The word *that* stipulates that the *specific thing* asked for in accordance with the condition will be granted.

Verse 14 restates the same condition in slightly different terminology: "If ye shall ask any thing in my name, I will do it." As in the previous verse, Christ fully expected the disciples to pray in this fashion with the guarantee that the response would be just as definite: "I will do it." This time, however, the emphasis is upon the fact that Christ Himself will answer the request. I say this because in the original Greek text the word *I* is emphasized.

This passage reveals that in some sense *God conditions His actions on human asking.* I don't fully understand the mechanics of it, but I certainly believe it! We have presented here for the first time a new "in my name" relationship from which a believer can petition effectively. "If ye shall ask . . . I will do it" seems to be in the nature of divine-human partnership. I have a part and Christ has a part. The language indicates that I am responsible to ask in His name; and if I ask, then He is equally responsible to do! This seems to be more than a creator-creature or master-servant relationship. It's a copartnership —a partnership of activity and achievement!

Jesus emphatically announced to His disciples that He had chosen them (*see* John 15:16). Following this announcement, two purpose clauses are given: ". . . that ye should go and bring forth fruit . . ." and ". . . that whatsoever ye shall ask . . ." (verse 16). These two clauses are parallel, and they state the reasons for their appointment by Christ. Christ chose them that they should be productive or fruit-

ful, and that they should obtain such answers to prayer as would make
them fruitful.

Of importance to this study is the fact that clearly prayer is associated with productivity (fruitbearing) even as it had been associated with doing greater works in the passage we just considered
(*see* John 14:12). Biblical evidence increasingly indicates that Christian activity is to be accomplished by our asking and God doing.

The same conditions of prayer stated in John 14:13, 14 are repeated.
The promise is again universal ("whatsoever") and conditioned by
asking "in my name." This time the disciples are instructed to direct
their requests specifically to the Father, and in this instance the Father
is also designated as the One granting the request. This differs from
the previous promise in John 14:13 where Christ Himself is said to
be the One who will grant the believer's request. Thus both Christ and
the Father are seen as expeditors of the prayers of believers.

The prayer condition is once again stated in a way that indicates
Christ fully expected the disciples to meet the condition (more probably future condition). The grammar indicates that in each individual
case in which the disciples ask the Father, He will correspondingly
give. Thus Jesus intended His disciples to have a fruitful ministry, but
prayer was to be the means by which that fruit would be produced.

In John 16:23,24 the Lord reveals explicitly what has been implicit
in all of His statements relative to praying in His name up to this point
—prayer in His name is a privilege specifically for the time after our
Lord ascended and the Holy Spirit descended. The expression "in that
day" (John 16:23) refers to the new age which began at Pentecost.

The next words are somewhat puzzling: ". . . ye shall ask me
nothing" (verse 23). The words can either mean, "Ask me no questions," or "Make no petitions." Most commentators agree that the
phrase indicates that in the new age there would be no need to
personally ask the visible Christ for anything. It should be noted that
in the original text the word *me* is heavily emphasized. This gives a
clear contrast between asking "me" and asking "the Father in my
name" (verse 23). For three years the disciples had freely asked Jesus
whenever needs arose, but with the new age, this would no longer be
necessary because they would then have the privilege of asking the

Father in His name! Does this not indicate a new and drastic distinction between the days of Christ's earthly sojourn and the age of grace that began at Pentecost? And does not that distinction involve a distinction in prayer practice? It most certainly seems to if we let the language speak for itself.

This evident distinction is made even clearer by the insertion of the phrase "Verily, verily" (verse 23), because it emphasizes the significance of what is to be said. Thus, asking the Father "in my name" seems to be a bold advance in Jesus' prayer teaching; a bold advance which will be realized "in that day" (the present age).

To heighten the concept of a dramatic advance even further, the Lord adds, "Hitherto have ye asked nothing in my name" (verse 24). It is difficult to see this as anything less than an advance on the disciple's former knowledge and experience of prayer. Here a new prayer plateau has been reached. The disciples are being given a higher illumination in the fine art of prayer. The expression "hitherto" means literally "until now," the idea being that up to that point in time the disciples had *never* prayed in the fashion Christ was herein advocating (asking in His name). But when the new age began, they would most certainly begin to pray that way.

Now we have seen that the disciples had most certainly prayed prior to this announcement. They had long since been taught to direct their prayers to the Father (*see* Luke 11:1–4), but they had never yet prayed "in my name"! The mighty John the Baptist knew nothing of praying in this fashion! None of the greats of the Old Testament ever experienced this kind of prayer! I'm sure you can see that whatever "in my name" asking involves, it is a privilege unknown to men of God prior to the formation of the New Testament Church on the day of Pentecost ("that day"). And whatever it is, it really packs a wallop because it will enable the disciples to be fruitful and do greater works!

The announcement of this new prayer privilege is followed by a command to ask (*see* John 16:24). The command is voiced in a tense that points up the fact that the continuous habit should be to petition in this fashion. Following the command is the typical promise ". . . ye shall receive . . ." (verse 24). The tense indicates a positive assurance that the prayer offered in this manner will be answered *for*

sure! Finally, the reason the Father will answer "in my name" praying is designated: ". . . that your joy may be full" (verse 24). The
phrase indicates not only a fact but an abiding state also.

The Lord explains that hereafter there will be an increased clarity
of revelation (*see* verse 25), and this fullness of knowledge will lead
to a fuller prayer privilege. The time in which this greater prayer
privilege will be exercised is once again designated as "that day" (John
16:26), which, as seen previously, is a reference to the new era initiated
at Pentecost. Approaching the Father in the name of the Son was to
be the hallmark of their higher privileges in the new age. Prayer in
His name, then, seems to be indicative of prayer based upon a new
relationship which would begin on the day of Pentecost. Otherwise,
why delay asking in His name until "that day"?

The drastic nature of this new advance in prayer privilege is heightened by the Lord's next words: ". . . I say not unto you, that I will
pray the Father for you" (verse 26). Clearly the reference is to the
personal praying of Jesus Himself as seen by the emphatic use of the
word *I* and must refer to *intercession* since the petitions are "for you."

Christ is thus stating that in view of the new prayer privilege
inaugurated by the new age, His own personal intercession concerning
the disciples will, in some sense, not be necessary. Evidently, prior to
Pentecost the petitions of the disciples needed the personal prayers of
Jesus to authenticate them—much as a memo to the president of a
company would need the personal validation of the foreman before it
could be cleared to go to the head man. Now Christ says you won't
need His validation on your prayers because you can address the
Father *directly* in His name. Certainly, to say the very least, this infers
a *radical* change in prayer relationships.

Meaning of "In My Name"

Our analysis of these four passages makes one fact very evident:
Whatever it may involve, prayer in His name is of tremendous significance! It seems limitless in its possibilities and privileges. But what
does it really mean to pray in His name? If the books and commentaries are any indication, it could be seriously doubted whether any real

understanding of the concept can be had at all! Yet strangely Jesus never seemed to feel that it was necessary to define what asking in His name involved. Also, His disciples never displayed any bewilderment over the concept. You can be sure, however, that the disciples were capable of asking Christ for clarification when they did not understand what He meant. In fact, right in this very discourse both Peter and Thomas interrupted Him with a question (*see* John 13:36–38 and 14:5–7). The Apostle Peter had a question mark for a brain! So you can be absolutely sure that if those men had had the slightest question as to what our Lord meant by praying in His name, they would have fired questions at Him. The *absence* of any question argues strongly that those Jewish disciples completely understood what it meant to ask in His name! I think the key to understanding this obviously potent prayer concept is to try and project ourselves back into that culture and view it from a first-century Jewish perspective.

In light of the fact that our Lord bears well over a hundred titles, how are we to determine which name is indicated by the "in my name" idea? Some men go to considerable lengths to show that praying in His name must refer to a specific title: Jesus, Lord, Christ, etc. However, such an approach misses the significance of the expression "name" as understood by the Jewish mind. Generally where no title is mentioned, no title is intended! Thus the very fact that in all six references to prayer in His name, no specific title is mentioned or intimated, argues strongly that the concept simply does not involve a title! The concept intended by "name" lies in another direction.

Christ evidently did not intend the phrase "in my name" to be a fixed formula attached to a prayer. Had this been His purpose, He surely would have so indicated and would have plainly identified the correct title to use: "in Jesus' name," "in Emmanuel's name," "in Christ's name," etc! Furthermore, it is strikingly significant that of all the prayers recorded in the Book of Acts and the Epistles, not one of them closes with a fixed terminology incorporating a name. Does this mean that the Apostles and early Christians didn't pray in His name? Hardly!

Thus praying in His name is *not* ending your prayers with a fixed phrase, "this we ask in Jesus' name." It is not a rabbit's foot to hang on the end of a prayer to give it punch! Now I'm not saying that a Christian is necessarily sinning when he closes his prayer in such a fashion. What I am saying is that simply reciting those words does not guarantee you are in reality praying in His name! The concept is far deeper and more significant than a formula with which to cap off a prayer!

What precisely did the Lord mean? To a Westerner, a name is usually a convenient device for identifying one individual from another. However, to the Easterner in the first century, a name signified far more. Indeed, one of the purposes of a name was to express some outstanding quality possessed by the individual. Sometimes the name described the nature of the person. At other times it pointed to circumstances surrounding his birth. It could even refer to the person's appearance.

The name given to God represented the Hebrew peoples' idea of the character of that God, or the relation God had with them. The name of God was synonymous with the Person of God. So when those Jewish disciples heard Jesus command them to ask in His name, neither Peter, nor Thomas, nor any of them were puzzled in the least bit. Why? Because they were already familiar with the basic connotation of the word *name*.

Thus, in using the expression "name," Christ was undoubtedly signifying the idea of *being, personality,* and *character.* The name of Christ stands for Christ Himself! By way of example, what does the Bible mean when it tells us to believe "in the name of the only begotten Son of God" (John 3:18)? Does it not mean to believe in the *Person* of Christ? Does it not mean to rest by faith in all that Christ is, has done, and will do? Thus to ask in Christ's name is to petition on the basis of all that Christ is, has done, is doing, and will yet do!

With all of this in mind, it should not be forgotten that the preposition *in* carries the root idea of "sphere." Hence the phrase "in my name" may be freely translated, "in the sphere of my name." Thus to pray "in my name" conveys the concept of praying in the sphere of Christ's total Person—His ownership, protection, presence, power, glory, etc.

And why can we now pray "in the sphere of His name"? Because, since the day of Pentecost, every believer has been "in Christ." On that day, by virtue of the baptizing ministry of the Holy Spirit, every believer was placed into the spiritual (yet real) body of Christ (*see* Acts 1:5; *compare* 1 Corinthians 12:13).

There is now a mystical union between Christ and the believer which is at once representative, organic, vital, supernatural, and indissoluble in nature. Christ and the believer have the same life. They are not separate persons linked together by some tenuous bond of friendship, but rather they are united in a tie as close as if the same blood ran in their veins! To pray in His name, then, is tantamount to praying on the basis of this new relationship. It is to pray from the vantage point of our new and exalted position in Christ!

It was for this reason that the disciples were told that the privilege of asking in His name was reserved for the new age that was to begin at Pentecost! Prior to Pentecost, none had or could ask in His name. To ask in His name demanded that they first be placed into Christ.

Today every believer is in the Body and has the privilege of asking in His name, but this does not mean that every believer is availing himself of that privilege! Nor does it mean that all of the prayers of all Christians since Pentecost have been "in my name" prayers. As with every divine blessing and privilege, it must be appropriated by faith. Thus to really pray in His name is not to mumble some little formula at the conclusion of your prayer but to petition fully conscious of who you are in Christ! It's to ask really *believing* that you are in Christ! It's one thing to be in Christ, and it's another to fully realize and believe it!

A very prominent concept involved with "in my name" praying is that of authority. If I'm in Christ and can petition on that basis, then I can ask with His authority! When Peter said confidently to a lame man outside the Temple, "In the name of Jesus Christ . . . rise up and walk" (Acts 3:6), he was in effect saying, "By the authority of Jesus Christ, rise up and walk." Today I can ask the Father for things with all the authority of Christ because I'm in Christ!

Concluding Thoughts on Prayer Conditions

It should be readily apparent that all three conditions are, in a real sense, various aspects of submission to the divine will. Faith is a trusting confidence in God and His will. Abiding is the deliberate, willful maintenance of an unbroken, vital communion between the believer and Christ which, of necessity, involves a basic submission to Christ. To fully realize and believe that one is in Christ automatically brings about a conformity to Him. Hence a person really praying *in His name* will pray with His motives and in accord with His character. Thus even the condition "in my name" necessitates a basic conformity to divine will. Unless God has clearly and definitely stated His will in the Scripture, we have no right to pray for anything without saying or implying, "Thy will be done." No human will was ever intended to stifle or frustrate God's holy will. The old adage "Prayer changes things" is certainly true in a very legitimate sense. However, it certainly does not mean that prayer changes God or His will! The truth of Scripture is that God is ever using all things (including prayer) to transform us so that we are increasingly realizing *in His will* the greatest possible joy in human life (*see* Romans 8:28). If we look at prayer in this fashion, we will not fall into the trap of viewing it as the annihilation of the human will, but rather the annihilation of all that is selfish in the human will! To insist that all legitimate prayer be in accord with divine will does not limit our petitions to the expressed will of God as seen in the Bible. The expressions "whatsoever" and "all things whatsoever" clearly demonstrate the limitless possible prayer petitions *within* God's will.

Perhaps today we need to get back to the basic biblical method of believers consistently asking and God effectively moving. Some dear folk are always looking for new methods or more organization. Now, I suppose there is an element of truth in it all, but so often the church simply ends up spinning her wheels. When all of the promotional dust has settled, no ground has really been gained. I'm personally convinced that what is needed is less *organizing* and more *agonizing;* less clever methodology and more fervent asking. This certainly is the battle plan outlined by Christ in the Upper Room.

Christ also revealed that the ultimate goal of prayer is the glory of God. As things are accomplished in response to prayer, God thereby looks good! God's reputation is enhanced. Yet Christ also stated that successful praying has the reflex action of bringing a fullness of joy to the person whose prayers are answered. I'm sure any prayer warrior can identify with this. You've spent weeks laboring in earnest prayer over a specific matter. Then suddenly God answers in a marvelous manner. There is a joyous elation filling your heart that is comparable only to the thrill of leading a sinner to the Saviour.

PART FOUR
THE PRAYER PRINCIPLES OF JESUS

In the first three sections we have been viewing the phenomenon of prayer in its actual setting in the Gospel. In this last section we are going to arrange this rather large mass of material topically because the human mind more readily comprehends truth when it is laid out in an orderly fashion. If my statements seem somewhat dogmatic and unsupported, remember that biblical proof has already been carefully presented in the previous parts. All we are trying to do is discuss what prayer was, as Jesus taught it, and what He said it could do.

15
The Significance, Nature, and Content
of Prayer

Three important areas will be dealt with in this chapter that will hopefully enable us to appreciate what prayer really was to our Lord Jesus Christ.

The Significance of Prayer

Every indication points to the fact that prayer was considered by Jesus a key factor (if not *the* key factor) in accomplishing God's work on this earth.

Prayer crowned both the beginning and ending of His public ministry (baptism and ascension). Prayer marked each significant juncture of His earthly program. No important decision was made without resorting to prayer. Jesus never allowed anything to interfere with prayer. He prayed regardless of the inconvenience of the hour or the pressing schedule of daily activities. Prayer was a *must* for Christ. No subject pertaining to the practical aspects of daily living received greater attention.

Jesus' instructions on the subject of prayer are full and extensive. Prayer is pictured as the necessary ingredient to ward off such serious threats as temptation and discouragement. Prayer is advocated when the pressures become so intense that we are prone to give up or cave in. It is to be the means of arriving at proper decisions.

The significance of prayer is especially evident in Christ's final high-level discussion with His key men, referred to as the Upper Room Discourse. He clearly states that divine action is, in some manner, conditioned upon human asking (*see* John 14:13, 14). In the ministry of prayer the believer is pictured as an active partner with God. In this partnership we are to petition and God is to perform.

This is the way the work of the church on earth is to be accomplished! It is not to be accomplished primarily by organization or clever administration, though they certainly have their place. Even preaching needs to be bathed in fervent prayer because to be effective the Gospel must go forth not in word only but in power as well. Mysteriously, God's power is mediated through prayer. Jesus clearly taught that the disciples were powerless because they were prayerless (*see* Mark 9: 29).

In light of Jesus' life and teachings, it is impossible to imagine a Christian really functioning successfully apart from a vital prayer life. By the same token it is impossible to envision a church functioning effectively apart from consistent, fervent prayer. Yet I'm afraid the evidence indicates that this is precisely the case for most churches and most Christians! A year ago at the opening session of the Greater Los Angeles Sunday School Association Convention, several thousand ministers, Sunday-school superintendents, Sunday-school teachers, and lay leaders were gathered together for a mass rally. At the conclusion of his address, the speaker had the audience bow their heads. Then he asked everyone who had consistently spent an average of thirty minutes in prayer each day to raise their hands. The speaker reported that less than five percent of the audience raised their hands! Think of it—the cream of the evangelical community in the Greater Los Angeles area, and less than five percent of them spent even thirty minutes a day on their faces before God! Then we wonder why nothing happens! In that same convention there were seminars on everything from visual aids to demonism, but so far as I could determine, there wasn't even one on how to pray effectively!

Recently a young man working on his doctor's degree toured the United States studying churches all over the country. A friend of mine asked him what there was to be found in common among churches in America. Without hesitation he responded, "Lack of prayer." Let's face it. The deadest service in most churches is the midweek prayer service! Often it's really a Bible study with prayer as an incidental appendage! Do you want victory? Pray! Do you honestly want action? Pray! Do you want your church to really *move?* Pray! That's God's method. You ask and He will do!

The Nature of Prayer

What was prayer as it was actually practiced and taught by Jesus Christ? I think the flavor of New Testament prayer can be stated in several propositions.

Prayer Is an Act

Recently there has been a rash of literature flooding the evangelical market wherein prayer is pictured as a short of nebulous communal *attitude.* We are being told that so long as a person is in this frame of mind he is engaged in prayer. Now I am certainly not opposed to a person being in an attitude of communion with God. Beyond question Jesus, in His waking hours, was always in a communal attitude with the Father. However, the facts of Scripture indicate that Jesus was not *always* praying! For Jesus, prayer was a definite, precise act, never merely an attitude. It had stated times of beginning and ending.

I have deliberately looked for biblical support in the writings of those who advocate prayer as an attitude. The only passage they utilize is Paul's statement "Pray without ceasing" (1 Thessalonians 5:17). The argument seems to be that a person could not literally be ceaselessly engaged in the *act* of prayer, so Paul must be referring to an *attitude* of prayer. But every indication in the New Testament points to prayer as an act, so how can we interpret this one passage in a manner that is out of harmony with prayer as uniformly presented? This is a poor interpretation.

Not only is the interpretation poor but it is also contrary to the realities of life! Even if Paul's command could be taken as an attitude, it is obvious that it could not be carried out in an *absolute* sense! Nobody, not even Paul, could maintain an attitude twenty-four hours a day! Certainly when Paul slept he could not maintain such an attitude! Obviously Paul's command is to be taken in a relative sense. Paul is saying that prayer should be such an integral part of our lives that throughout each day we should be carrying on a running conversation with God. Each problem, each decision, each difficulty should occasion a brief prayer. It is not necessary to get on your knees or even bow your head. Right at your desk you can pray. While pumping gas, pray! Driving down the freeway, shoot up short prayers as needs and situations arise. Prayer ought to be our instant and first recourse all during the day. This is what Paul means by "Pray without ceasing."

As I said at the outset of this discussion, I'm certainly not opposed to maintaining a communal attitude with God. In fact, all effective prayer must be voiced in the context of such an attitude. However, never confuse the *attitude* with the *act* of prayer. As we have already seen, Jesus taught rather extensively about the importance of having a proper heart attitude when one engages in prayer. Yet in all His instruction He *never* confused attitude with act. He never equated attitude with prayer. They were always distinct.

Prayer Is Essentially an Act of Petition

Before I started studying about prayer in the Bible and had simply read books, written by men, about prayer, I was led to believe that a good prayer had to start with adoration. Then, after one adored God for a while, he must next engage in confession. Following a time of confession, a good prayer would proceed to thanksgiving. Finally after adoration, confession, and thanksgiving, one got around to supplication! The impression was that you first had to butter God up with adoration and thanksgiving. Then when you had Him good and buttered up, you got around to what you were really after in the first place —*to ask God for things!* May I say that you will never find this sweet little prayer formula in the Gospels!

The prayer sessions of Jesus, almost without exception, arose from crisis situations wherein our Lord was driven to voice petitionary needs to the Father. His major prayers were all centered around requests. His nonpetitionary prayers were usually found in such routine activities as blessing food, blessing children, or spontaneous outbursts of praise and thanksgiving. But this type of praying constituted the exception rather than the rule. Jesus' general practice was to launch immediately into petitions after a brief word of address to the Father. In the overwhelming majority of His prayers there was never praise, thanksgiving, or adoration as such.

Jesus also taught prayer as a petition. Prayer was asking, seeking, and knocking. Probably the most graphic example of this was the rather extensive teaching session Jesus gave in response to a specific request: "Lord, teach us to pray . . ." (Luke 11:1). Now what did Jesus teach them? He first cited a model prayer consisting of six petitions which demonstrated what types of things they might legitimately request in prayer (*see* Luke 11:2–4).

Next, He launched into a parable which gave them an illustration of the attitude which men should manifest when they petition the Father (*see* verses 5–8). Following this, He explicitly commanded the disciples to persistently ask, seek, and knock (*see* verses 9, 10).

Finally He gave them an analogy to indicate what type of answers they could expect from the Father if they petitioned in this manner (*see* verses 11–13). Thus, in response to a request, "Lord, teach us to pray," Jesus gave an extended discourse on how to effectively ask God for things!

Looking back to Jesus' more lengthy prayers, a conversational element can, indeed, be found. However, the conversational material is interwoven throughout the prayer in the form of explanatory material. Clearly the chief function of what might be termed "conversation" in Jesus' prayers served the purpose of explanation, argumentation, and elucidation concerning the petitions. Jesus' habit was to voice a petition and then extensively explain *why* the petition was given and precisely *what* was intended by it. The conversation existed, to be sure, but it was *conversation with a purpose,* and more accurately *conversation with a petitionary purpose.* Remove the petitions from Jesus' prayers and the conversational elements are largely meaningless.

What I'm trying to get across is that a Christian should never be afraid of asking God for things. You can never ask Him too often or for too much! God loves to have you make requests of Him. Don't feel that you are praying amiss if you only petition during times of special heartache. At such times it is far better to just pour out your soul in agonized petition than to artificially precede your petition with praise just to make the prayer seem "proper." God knows when you're faking it. He knows when your thanksgiving is simply an "add on" to make the prayer appear pious. When your heart is breaking, cry out to Him. That's really what God loves for us to do.

Prayer Is an Act of Specific Petition

Christ's petitions were always precise and specific. When He asked the Father for glory, He carefully specified the particular type of glory intended. When He interceded for someone, He carefully explained what He wanted the Father to do for that particular person and why. When He prayed on behalf of a group of people He was always careful to define the group and the exact request He was making on their behalf. The same thing could be said of the prayers in the Epistles.

The New Testament knows nothing of vague, generalized asking! Yet so often our prayers are for generalities. You know what I mean: "God bless my church," or "God bless the missionaries!" Why do we pray this way? Some say it is due to a basic lack of faith. When we ask for specific things it puts our faith on the line. It is very easy to know when and if God answers, but if we pray in vague generalities, we "hedge our bet," so to speak. It takes little faith to ask God to bless the missionaries because then any blessing can be considered an answer to prayer. However, to ask God to do a specific thing for a specific missionary taxes one's faith and is very readily verified. Thus, subconsciously we tend to say, "I had better allow God a little leeway!"

However, it has been my observation that the real reason behind vague asking is lack of vital concern! I've noticed that whenever I am really burdened about a matter I get very specific as to what I want God to do about it. Conversely, when I'm not really concerned and am just going over my prayer list because that's the pious thing to do, I become extremely vague in my asking. There is a direct correlation between the level of concern and degree of preciseness in asking. Jesus was always concerned when He prayed and, therefore, was always precise.

Prayer Is an Act of Urgent Petition

Obviously this concept ties in with our previous discussion as to the reason for vague petitions. Christ was not only specific in His asking but He was always in dead earnest as well. His petitions invariably arose from a sense of need created by a crisis. The actual wording of the prayers themselves pointed to urgent need as the prompting factor. Likewise, when Christ taught prayer, His parables and illustrations were set in a background of crisis which, in turn, created a need and prompted earnest petition. Prayer was taught against a background of such things as a man desperately pounding on a neighbor's door, or a deeply troubled widow, driven by dire need to appeal to an unjust judge.

A person in trouble will not only pray but he will also pray in dead earnest. A man with his car stalled on the railroad tracks with a train approaching won't look upon prayer as a nice religious exercise. I'm sure we can all testify to the fact that our most effective times of prayer have been when we've been in big trouble. Remember how effectively you prayed in the ambulance as they were rushing your child to the emergency room at the hospital? The only problem is that *we are always in trouble,* but we are too blind to realize it! Each day we are involved in a titanic struggle with unseen yet real forces (*see* Ephesians 6:12). We are called upon to do battle daily with the world, the flesh, and the devil. We've got the world that's *external,* the flesh that's *internal,* and the devil who's *infernal* to deal with every day of our lives!

If we could actually see the hellish hordes around us each day, we would be panicked into fervent prayer! For this reason I have found it profitable to cry out, "Lord, open my eyes. Help me to be sensitive to my real dangers as well as the needs of my friends." Until you are convinced of a need, you will not pray with urgency, and unless you pray with urgency, you are not *really praying!* To be sure, the degree of earnestness and urgency will vary, but it will always be present in biblical praying. It is for this reason that much of what we call praying today is not really prayer at all. We are just playing religious games under the pretense of a prayer time. The sad thing is that we seldom really get down to business in prayer! I dare say there are Christians who haven't really prayed in years, and we wonder why God is not moving among us!

Prayer Is an Act of Emotional Petition

Because prayer, by nature, is essentially an act of urgent, specific petition generally arising out of a crisis situation, it logically follows that it is emotionally wrought. The deepest and most profound emotions were displayed by Christ while He was in the act of prayer. Beyond question, Christ's prayer life gives one the clearest possible insight into His emotional makeup as He walked this earth. Because Christ prayed as a man, the emotions displayed were typically human. There was absolutely no warrant for emotionless, ritual praying in the prayer life of Jesus Christ.

In His prayers the entire gamut of emotions can be seen. They reach from the heights of almost ecstatic joy to the depths of unimaginable emotional turmoil. The more emotionally disturbed our Lord became, the more fervently He prayed. The frequent, short, spontaneous prayer outbursts give testimony not only to the frequency but also to the emotional setting of Christ's prayers. Good news as well as bad news prompted prayer.

The greatest insight into the emotional backdrop out of which Jesus' prayer life sprang is found in the Garden of Gethsemane. In that instance Christ's emotionally depressed state reached a point where it affected His very countenance and he fell prostrate on the ground, sweating great drops of blood!

The emotional factor is also evident in His teachings. Praying is given as a recommendation in lieu of fainting. Prayer is commanded even while the enemy is in the act of persecuting the believer. Can you picture a Christian mouthing prayers with no emotion while being beaten over the head with a bat? Legitimate prayer is pictured as a man completely downcast, beating his breast. It's impossible to contemplate a man under such conditions not being emotionally involved. The degree of emotional involvement can vary from prayer to prayer. The way emotions are expressed varies from person to person. However, emotions will always be involved in true prayer. So pray when you are glad and pray when you are mad—and pray at every stage in between.

Prayer Is an Act of Filial Petition

One final word needs to be said with regard to the nature of prayer. It is an act of *filial* petition. Remember the word *filial* means an intimate child-parent relationship. At the very foundation of Jesus' concept of prayer was the direct address of the soul to God *as Father.* Only once, in all of His recorded prayers, did He fail to address God as Father, and that was the tormented cry from the cross, "My God, my God, why hast thou forsaken me?" (Matthew 27:46).

His prayer instructions repeatedly emphasized this truth. Beginning with His first prayer teachings in the Sermon on the Mount, and continuing through His last, in the Upper Room, He consistently instructed that prayer be addressed directly to God as Father. As noted several times previously in this book, this was a radical departure from both Jewish and pagan practice. It carried a sense of intimacy unknown in prayer concepts up to that time. No Jew would have dared address Jehovah as Father.

The intimacy is intensified when one realizes that Jesus used the Aramaic word *Abba* which carries the idea of a small child addressing his parent. As noted earlier, it conveyed the idea of "Daddy" or "Papa." This is a beautiful concept. By addressing our prayer to God as Father, we recognize Him as immediately related to us personally. Think of it! I am personally related to the God of heaven and can call Him Father! As Father, God concerns Himself personally, directly, and constantly with the welfare of His children. Therefore, when I pray, I am not calling upon some awesome Being way out there, but to a Father, in all the best connotation of that term. He is my Father, the One who loves me with a love that is always wise, pure, unselfish, and perfect. I can pour out my soul to my Father because He understands me perfectly. I can be free and uninhibited with Him, for no one is stiff and formal with a daddy. Yet in all this we must remember that "Father" also carries the idea of respect.

The Content of Prayer

Content, strangely, was never emphasized in Christ's teachings on prayer. Jesus placed the chief emphasis on the petitionary character and the proper attitude in prayer. Aside from the Lord's Prayer, we are left almost totally to a study of Jesus' personal prayers for any hint as to what should be included in prayer content.

The fact that specific teaching on the content of prayer is rather sparse when compared with the abundance of material on prayer attitudes leads to the inevitable conclusion that *what* is said in prayer is not nearly so important as *how* (with what attitude) it is said.

Extent of Content

The many invitations in Christ's prayer teachings that involve the words *anything* and *whatsoever* make it apparent that prayer can legitimately be voiced for anything great or small, material or immaterial, that is consistent with the revealed nature of God. God is concerned with those issues that concern His people. No domain of the believers' life and interests need be excluded from the scope of prayer. Every detail of life may be made an object of prayer.

After all, if the Father is the kind of person our Lord taught us He is, then nothing can be too big to bring before Him. Nothing need be considered too tough for Him to tackle. If He is capable of removing mountains and raising the dead, He is certainly capable of doing anything you might ask Him to do, if it's for your good and His glory.

Conversely, nothing need be considered too small or too trivial to bring before our heavenly Father. After all, did not Jesus teach us that the Father has the very hairs of our head numbered? Is He not aware when even a sparrow falls to the ground? If He is this kind of God, I can feel free to bring the most insignificant matters before Him. Things that are sometimes called "trifles" often have a far-reaching significance. Therefore, there need be no hesitation in laying before Him such matters. Never feel that the Father is too important or too busy to be bothered with small issues.

Yet, having said all this, it is an inescapable fact that Jesus in His own personal prayers *always* prayed concerning matters that were obviously significant. The same could also be said of the prayers of Paul in the Epistles. Jesus never prayed for obvious trivialities. For example, Jesus never prayed, "Father, help Me to find a parking place," or "Father, help me to win a Ping-Pong game." Now I'm not saying that it is wrong to pray for such things. I'm simply pointing out the fact that matters of this nature never appear in the prayers of

Jesus. So if eighty percent of our praying pertains to such matters, can we claim to be praying in the spirit of Jesus?

In a world with such dire needs, in a world where men are daily going to hell, there is something tragic about spending a significant portion of our praying with such matters as Ping-Pong games and parking places. By way of example, suppose you were invited to the White House to have a personal interview with the president, and at the conclusion of the interview the president said, "My friend, I would like to do something for you. What would you like? Just ask me for anything and if it's within my power as president, I will grant it to you."

With this tremendous opportunity suppose you responded by saying, "Mr. President, would you give me a thirteen-cent postage stamp." Now there is nothing morally wrong with asking the president of the United States for a postage stamp, but I'm quite sure your friends back home would have a few well-chosen words for you! They would probably say, "With such a fantastic opportunity, all you asked for was a postage stamp?" I wonder if, at times, we don't do the same thing with the God of heaven.

Elements of Content

In His only major teaching on prayer content (the Lord's Prayer, Luke 11:1–4), there was an obvious division in the six petitions. The first three petitions pertained to the advancement of God's program —a program that would ultimately see God's name hallowed, God's kingdom established, and God's perfect will accomplished. Thus one important segment of prayer content ought to pertain to what might be termed petitions of *aspiration*—petitions that aspire (desire) to see God's purposes fully accomplished on this planet. This would include praying for missionaries, churches, and other agencies that are involved in carrying out the Great Commission. A person's normal prayer life should include a large amount of this type of petition.

The final three petitions of the Lord's Prayer turn from aspiration to more immediate personal concerns. These pertain to any legitimate physical or spiritual need. In the area of material needs, the fourth petition pertaining to "daily bread" (Luke 11:3) is so worded as to make prayer legitimate for all immediate material necessities, be they great or small. However, no warrant exists for requesting excessive material luxuries. It is "daily" bread, not a whole bakery. It is "bread," not cake.

The final two petitions in the Lord's Prayer pertain to the ever-present spiritual struggle with which every disciple must constantly cope. It is perfectly proper, and even necessary, for us to make urgent requests concerning our spiritual needs or the needs of our fellow believers. Virtually all of Christ's personal petitions pertained to spiritual problems (His own or those of His disciples). Requests for spiritual needs can include such items as protection from evil, forgiveness, sanctification, and cleansing. Seemingly prominent in Christ's own life was the petition for guidance. Evidence strongly indicates that the vast majority of our Lord's private sessions of prayer on mountaintops or in desert regions was motivated by a need for the Father's direction. At any rate, both by His example and by His teaching it is clear that a large segment of our prayer should be devoted to the crucial spiritual aspects of life.

Do you realize what an impact it would make on our spiritual development if we began to actually practice this? The average Christian is like Peter, who only cried out when he was about to drown in the sea of Galilee (*see* Matthew 14:28–31). The New Testament tells us to pray before we begin to sink. What victory we could enjoy if we saturated each day with instant prayers to the Father at every hint of trouble or danger. Try to reprogram your thinking about prayer. Try to get off the panic-prayer kick. Use prayer as a *first* resort rather than a *last* resort. To change lifelong prayer habits will not be easy, but I know you will find it well worth the effort.

Spiritual Emphasis in Content

The most striking fact about the content of prayer in the Gospels is the heavy emphasis upon the spiritual aspect. Aside from the fourth petition of the Lord's Prayer, our Lord never taught us to pray for material things. In actual practice Jesus rarely, if ever, prayed for material things, either for Himself or for others. He prayed that Peter's faith might not fail. He never prayed for Peter to get a better job. He prayed that the disciples might be kept from evil. He never prayed for them to get a new suit of clothes. He prayed for guidance, not for a better house.

The same can be said for the prayers of the Apostle Paul. He made it a habit to pray for the local churches. In those churches there were, in all probability, people who needed jobs, but Paul never prayed for jobs. In those churches there were folks who were falling behind in their mortgage payments, but he never prayed about such matters. By way of example, notice Paul's prayer on behalf of the local church at Colosse (*see* Colossians 1:9–11). Paul first prayed that they "might be filled with the knowledge of his will in all wisdom and spiritual understanding" (verse 9). When was the last time you prayed that a Christian brother might be filled with the knowledge of God's will in all wisdom and understanding? I want to tell you, friend, you can pray that prayer on my behalf anytime! I need it! Paul continued by praying that the Colossians "might walk worthy of the Lord . . ." (verse 10). He prayed that they might be "fruitful in every good work, and increasing in the knowledge of God" (verse 10). He prayed that they might be "Strengthened with all might . . ." (verse 11). Do you notice that they are all *spiritual needs?*

Jesus saw man's basic problem as spiritual, and His prayers reflect that insight. More and more I find myself putting a spiritual twist to my praying. When a brother is in the hospital with an infirmity, I still ask God to touch his body; but more and more I pray for the Lord's presence to be made real to him during this ordeal. I pray that his conduct and attitude in the hospital will be such that will glorify God. At times I will take Paul's prayer for the spiritual needs of the Philippians or Colossians and put a missionary's name at the beginning and pray for those very items on behalf of that missionary.

Organization of Content

Much of Jesus' praying seems to have been in the form of short, spontaneous outbursts as specific needs arose. Because of their brevity, it is impossible to detect anything by way of organization within their contents.

In Jesus' more lengthy recorded prayers, however, organization of some sort is always evident. The finest example of prayer organization is to be found in His High Priestly Prayer (*see* John 17). Christ begins by petitioning the Father on behalf of Himself. Next He moves to intercession on behalf of His immediate disciples, and finally on behalf of all disciples throughout this present age. The flow of thought is organized and moves smoothly and surely from one petition to another. Though all of our Lord's more lengthy prayers display some sort of organization, there is never an established organizational pattern.

There is never any indication that Jesus ever deliberately composed His prayers ahead of time. The fact is that the heavy emotional involvement evident in Jesus' prayers would argue against any type of prefabrication praying. After all, it's pretty hard to write out a prayer ahead of time and then read it with real emotion. How, then, do we account for the obvious organization evident in Jesus' prayers? The organization seems to come from a deep sense of need. The petitions Jesus voiced in His prayers represent the verbalization of issues that were of primary concern to our Lord. They were issues that were heavy on His heart which He had constantly mulled over in His mind. Thus they were matters that He had carefully thought out; and when it came time to pray, His prayers always had a certain organization to them.

I do not believe that Jesus ever got ready to pray and then said, "Let's see. What shall I bring before the Father today?" That's what we do and that's why our prayers are often disorganized. Jesus was constantly thinking about the program of God. His very life revolved around it. As this becomes increasingly true of us, our praying will take on more of an organizational quality. I know the times when my praying becomes very disjointed and disorganized are usually the times when there is no real burden on my heart, and no real concern. However, let a crisis appear on the horizon, and let me get really burdened about certain issues, and it's amazing how my prayers suddenly become organized. Why? Because during times of crisis, I'm constantly thinking about the problems involved. Therefore, when I pray, the issues are carefully thought out. All of this is simply another way of growing in grace. This involves being absorbed with the things of God daily. As this becomes true, our prayers will not only become more organized but more effective at the same time.

Elaborate, prefabricated, careless praying is not New Testament praying. New Testament praying is voiced by a man who is moving with God and His program. A man who is really absorbed in and concerned with God's purposes is a man who will inevitably have a certain built-in, organizational quality in his prayers.

Unusual Features of Content

Certain factors in the content of our Lord's prayers are quite unexpected and unusual, even mystifying in some instances. The phenomenal fact that only once did Jesus clearly instruct prayer concerning material things has already been extensively discussed.

Perhaps even more perplexing is the discovery that Jesus quite frequently voiced petitions pertaining to matters which were already providential certainties. By way of example, consider the second petition of the Lord's Prayer, "Thy kingdom come" (Luke 11:2). Now if anything is a lead-pipe cinch, it is the fact that God's kingdom shall indeed ultimately triumph! So why pray about such a matter? Yet this is precisely what Jesus taught. In fact, He not only taught it but He also practiced it! Why? To be very honest, we do not know for sure because God has not chosen to reveal the matter to us. However, even with our limited human mentality, perhaps we can come up with *possible* reasons.

First, by verbalizing a petition such as "Thy kingdom come" we invariably affirm an active faith in the fact that His kingdom will indeed, someday, be fully established. Second, by offering up such a request day by day, we are put in conscious harmony with the will and purpose of God. Third, by voicing petitions periodically for ultimate providential certainties, these prayers become sort of guideposts along the unknown way. We know that His kingdom will come but we are not sure exactly how and under what circumstances it will be set up. So by daily voicing such a petition, we drive a stake each day along the unknown path.

Totally unexpected is the large amount of prayer content devoted to Jesus' own personal needs. Jesus prayed *heavily* for Himself. Often He prayed *exclusively* for His own needs. In the High Priestly Prayer (*see* John 17), He began with a petition for Himself before interceding for His disciples. In the Lord's Prayer He advocated that one-half of the petitions be for the personal needs of the one praying. All of this certainly runs contrary to current notions on prayer. In fact, according to many contemporary authors, such praying would probably be labeled "selfish praying." Yet this is precisely the kind of prayer we find in the Gospels.

Almost shocking is the fact that Jesus *never* taught His followers *explicitly* to pray for the salvation of lost souls! Actually, little of Jesus' praying pertained directly to the unsaved. By and large His statement "I pray not for the world . . ." (John 17:9) holds true. The same emphasis can be seen in Paul's intercession! Paul had a passion for the souls of lost men to the end of his days, yet when he prayed, he concentrated on believers, not unbelievers.

One cannot escape the implication that the chief hindrance to evangelism is not the indifference of the harvest but the spiritual condition of the harvesters. Every great revival in history has begun with God's people getting *revived!* When God's people are spiritually "in shape," evangelism will be the natural and inevitable result. When the saints go forth in the power of the Holy Spirit, sinners will be won to Christ! Study the Wesleyan revivals in England, or the great revivals under Finney in our own country. This was always the pattern. Evangelism is the result of the saints getting revived! So long as the saints are spiritually inert, evangelism is blocked in a community.

In light of all this, it would be well for us to readjust our emphasis in evangelistic praying. Instead of so much praying for God to save the pigmies, would it not be well to pray more for the spiritual needs of those missionaries working among the pigmies? It would also be well to pray for God to thrust more spirit-filled laborers among the pigmies. While it is natural to pray for God to save our unsaved loved ones, it would be more in harmony with the New Testament pattern to also pray for God to thrust a spirit-filled believer across the path of that loved one!

16
Prayer Attitudes and Procedures

The Attitudes of Prayer

The major thrust of Christ's teachings on prayer centered in two areas: (1) the petitionary nature of prayer and (2) the proper heart attitude while praying. Jesus gave little attention to matters such as the position of the body, the duration of prayer, the place where prayers were to be offered, etc. With Jesus the crucial factor was not so much *what* one says in prayer or *how* eloquently it is said, but the *heart attitude* at the time he says it. A close relationship exists between proper heart attitude while praying and meeting the biblical conditions for having prayers answered. In fact it is impossible to have the proper heart attitude and not be meeting the biblical conditions for successful praying. In Jesus' prayer principles, six major attitudes come to light.

The first three attitudes are closely related. *Sincerity,* the foundational prayer attitude, was always reflected in Jesus' prayer life. Prayer was never perfunctory for our Lord. In His teachings on prayer the harshest possible words of rebuke were directed toward the hypocritical sham and insincerity of the religious leaders of that day. Jesus castigated prayer practices that were designed to make prayer a religious display wherein great piety was feigned for unworthy motives.

To counteract this, our Lord insisted on a basic seclusion in prayer. He likewise insisted that prayer be a direct, intimate address to our loving heavenly Father. In such circumstances the motives of sham and pretense are negated. What possible reason would a man have to enter a closet and address the Father in a hypocritical manner? Whom would he impress? Certainly such conduct would not impress the Father, and no one else would be aware of his actions.

Closely aligned with sincerity is the quality of *honesty.* Actually, it is quite impossible to exercise one without the other. A deep sincerity will eventuate in honesty. By way of example, the publican, in an attitude of deep sincerity which rendered him impervious to his surroundings, openly and honestly confessed his sin. Jesus taught that the Father is One who "seeth in secret" (Matthew 6:4) and is aware of every slight detail of our lives. Therefore, to enter a closet and address such a Being with dishonesty would be the sheerest possible folly. If you are not honest with Him when you pray, you are playing games and are certainly not praying. Just as honesty is the result of sincerity, so sincerity is motivated by *humility.* A humble man must be a sincere man and I'm talking about *true* humility. I don't mean the sickening kind of person who goes around with sort of a pained expression— the kind who has a "suffering for Jesus" look on his face.

A truly humbled person will be a submissive person with a humble, submissive heart which is a dependent heart. Dependency is the very core of biblical prayer. When you think about it, only a dependent creature truly prays.

This humble submission to God invariably begets unselfishness. No man can consciously voice a selfish petition and be humbly submissive to the Father at the same time. Jesus severely rebuked James and John when vengeful pride prompted a selfish prayer request. So the praying man is the humble man, and humility involves submissive dependence characterized by unselfishness.

Urgency, the fourth major prayer attitude, is extremely prevalent in the Gospels. It would be impossible for one accepting the integrity of the New Testament to seriously study the prayer life of Jesus Christ and fail to detect an underlying current of urgency throughout. The mood of the verbs, the context of crisis, in fact virtually every factor of Jesus' praying points to urgency.

His teaching also manifested the same undercurrent. All of His parables on prayer picture a person in trouble urgently desiring something. Praying is set over against fainting. Prayer is coupled with vigilant watching. The conclusion is overwhelming! If a man does not see a need which prompts some degree of urgency, he is not praying in the manner generally practiced and taught by Jesus. To be sure, the degree of urgency may vary, but to some degree it will always be present.

Closely associated with urgency is the matter of *earnestness*. A man urgently petitioning will invariably be a man earnestly petitioning. Christ always prayed with earnestness. Even while engaged in such a seemingly routine matter as blessing little children, He did it with an almost enthusiastic earnestness. Certainly there is never any real evidence that He ever performed an act of prayer as a careless ritual. No value is ever given to ritual petitions, even noble petitions rendered out of a sense of duty or propriety. If a man is not praying in earnest, he is not really praying.

The concept of *importunity* and dogged persistence is certainly one of the more emphasized and clearly delineated aspects of Jesus' teachings. Strangely, some men have tried to deny persistence in prayer altogether. They have argued that to ask over and over again for the same thing day after day is actually a demonstration of a lack of faith. It is contended that a person should ask God for something once and then quietly sit back in faith and wait for God to answer. Such thinking may be logical (on a human level), but it certainly is not biblical!

Christ went out of His way to teach persistence in asking. In two major parables (the friend at midnight and the unjust judge), this concept was clearly, precisely, and definitely set forth. In both parables a situation is envisioned wherein the petitioner is placed in desperate circumstances. A person in desperate need will be both shameless and persistent in his petitions. Jesus proceeded to instruct His followers to petition the Father as the desperate persons pictured in the parables did.

Perhaps this is one issue that needs to be clarified. We must never confuse persistent petition with vain repetitions. Christ taught the former but forbade the latter. Vain repetitions involve the fallacious concept that God will be heard by much speaking. A person engaged in this kind of praying actually thinks that by aimlessly repeating a prayer numerous times it becomes effective. To repeat the prayer twenty times is considered more effective than repeating it two times. This is the philosophy behind the Tibetan prayer wheel. A prayer is written out on a piece of paper and slipped into a notch on the wheel. Each time the wheel revolves the prayer is supposedly lifted into the presence of the god. This represents vain repetitions in the raw.

There are many subtle forms in which Christians, at times, can find themselves engaged in vain repetition. Certainly it is difficult to use so-called prayer beads without falling into the vain-repetition trap. Prayer lists used simply as a crutch to fill up time have also caused many a Christian inadvertantly to fall into the snare. Now I'm certainly not blasting prayer lists as such; but if a prayer list becomes a convenient device which allows you to aimlessly mouth over petitions with your mind almost in neutral, it comes very close to vain repetitions.

Persistent petition is vastly different. Both persistent petition and vain repetitions involve the idea of repeating a request, but the motivation for each is different. Importunate asking is prompted by the very burden of the heart. It is driven by the force of an almost overpowering sense of urgency—an urgency which continues to cry out day after day.

Christ in the Garden of Gethsemane provides a classic example of this type of asking. At least three times in that prayer session our Lord cried out for the cup to be removed. However, it is obvious even to the casual reader that Christ was not keeping count as to how many times He repeated the petition. One never gets the impression that Christ was thinking, "I've given this petition three times; now if I can voice it twelve more times, it will really have the whammy." No, not at all. Christ was simply so burdened that He kept crying out for the cup to be removed, if at all possible! This is persistent petition at its finest. I'm sure you have had such a burden concerning a matter that you found yourself bringing it before the Father day after day without being at all aware of how often you voiced that desperate need. That, my friend, is persistent asking.

The fact that importunate prayer was actually taught by Christ is obvious, but why did He tell us to keep on asking for the same thing day after day? I can understand why delays are necessary. After all, God doesn't operate on the basis of my wristwatch. With His infinite wisdom, He knows full well when to grant my petition. But why not just quietly wait in faith for God's answer during the delay? Why should I keep on asking? To state it bluntly, we don't really know! God has never told us why He wants us to keep up persistent asking during the delay. He simply tells us to do it.

Christ did, however, make it abundantly clear that perseverance in prayer was *never* to wear God down or to cause Him in exasperation to grant the request. God is not playing hard-to-get. Prayer is not conquering God's reluctance but laying hold of His willingness. Importunity in prayer should never be looked upon as a means of changing God. God never needs to be made willing to grant the request.

Well, if it's not to change God, then maybe persistent prayer is intended to change us! After all, when a solution to a problem is sought, at least two basic truths must be kept in mind. First, the person who has the answer must be willing to give it; second, the person who is seeking the answer must be able to receive it. Obviously the first truth is self-evident. Hence I am personally convinced that importunity is one of the tools God uses in developing us. Persistence in prayer is not to make God more like man but to make man more like God.

The same rational objections leveled against persistent asking could just as well be brought against diligent study! Why does God command us to study the Bible (*see* Timothy 2:15)? Is God not capable of immediately conveying all the information contained in the Bible without any effort on our part? Certainly God is capable of giving us information. He could instantly teach us the Hebrew and Greek language if He so willed. But the simple fact is that God doesn't choose to operate that way. He has ordained that biblical information be conveyed essentially by study on our part. Just as God grants some things through diligent study, He grants other things by persistent asking. In the final analysis we will discover that both the diligence of study and the discipline of asking are tools our Father uses to conform us to the image of Jesus Christ.

Perseverance can conceivably have the effect of separating deep-seated desire from momentary whim. By way of example, I have never actually attended a Rose Bowl game. I would like to see one, and I could attend one this next year. All I would have to do is take my bedroll over to the ticket office the night before tickets go on sale and spend the entire night on the sidewalk. Now, I would like to see a Rose Bowl game, but I don't want to see one *that* badly! So it is with some petitions. We would like to see God do many things, but only those things we deeply desire will we be willing to persistently bring before Him week in and week out.

Persistence in prayer has a definite tendency to purify a person's petitions. By daily verbalizing our petitions, our desires are either confirmed or condemned. It is almost impossible to voice a request day after day and not distinguish any unworthy qualities that might exist in the request. Thus we either modify the petition or get rid of it. Along the same line, persistence has a tendency to purify the person voicing the petition. How can a person present his most secret desires daily to God and not be purified in the process? If there are selfish motives involved in some of the requests, the very mechanics of verbalization will tend to bring this to the person's attention.

Beyond question, there are many other factors behind God's delayed answers to the prayers of His people. But behind all delay is the Person of God who loves to give good gifts to His children, and in some manner the delay is designed to benefit the praying disciple. God's "not yet" is ultimately utilized in the sanctifying process to bring us to the maturity of Christ.

Mysterious as it is, persistent struggle is a vital part of New Testament prayer. Lose the importunity of prayer, reduce it to simply conferring with God, lose the real sense of conflict, lose the habit of wrestling and the hope of prevailing, make prayer mere walking with God in friendly talk and, precious as it is, you tend to forfeit the reality of prayer in the end. In actuality, you make prayer mere conversation instead of the soul's great action. There is an inexplicable element of dogged struggle in biblical praying.

The Procedures of Prayer

A complex and rigid procedural structure for approaching God in prayer was never advocated by Jesus Christ. Aside from instruction concerning seeking solitude while praying and addressing prayer to the Father, nothing was directly taught about the procedural aspect of prayer. So far as the Gospels are concerned, the inclusion of certain mechanical details does not guarantee legitimate prayer. God attaches small importance to protocol if the heart is not right before Him. God responded to the cry of Peter as truly as He did to the long, formal prayer of Solomon at the dedication of the Temple.

With many non-Christian religions, it is the mechanics of prayer that are all-important: praying at a precise time of the day, facing a particular direction, assuming a certain position of the body, reciting a prescribed ritual prayer. The very opposite is true in biblical prayer. However, though they were secondary, Jesus did manifest certain procedural preferences in prayer. I believe we should be as biblical as possible even in these matters of secondary importance.

Times of Prayer. Jesus never taught a particular time for prayer. His habits revealed no specific preference for a designated hour of the day. While prayer was a distinct and vital part of the life of Jesus Christ and there can be no question but that He prayed often, His times of prayer seem to have been directed by *need* rather than *chronology.* We should and must pray, and must deliberately make time to pray. My current habit is to pray each morning in connection with my time of personal devotions. However, I am trying to develop the practice of praying intermittently during the day as needs arise and decisions are to be made, much as Paul referred to when he urged believers to be "instant in prayer" (Romans 12:12).

Jesus needed to pray and we need to pray. He often had to make time to pray and we must also! Satan will rarely allow times for prayer to be convenient. He knows how crucial they are!

Occasions of Prayer. As implied above, *occasion* for prayer has more significance in the principles of Jesus than does *time* of prayer. He initiated and concluded His public ministry with prayer. Often significant events in our Lord's ministry were preceded by a prayer session. He taught His disciples that men "ought always to pray . . ." (Luke 18:1). As we said earlier, crisis seemed to be the chief occasion for prayer. Crisis drove Jesus to prayer. The greater the crisis, the more intense was the prayer effort. Every difficulty, perplexity, and disillusionment should be an occasion for prayer.

Places of Prayer. Christ prayed in a great variety of locations. He prayed in desert regions, mountaintops, gardens, and city streets, the clear implication being that prayer can be offered from any geographical location. Indeed, if prayer can be effectively voiced by a condemned man hanging on a cross, location is irrelevant.

There are, however, strong indications that Christ preferred certain types of locale, if and when circumstances permitted. There is evidence that He had selected certain spots where He would habitually retreat for prayer. Yet the outstanding factor in prayer location evidenced both in His practice and preaching was that of seclusion. Mountains and deserts appealed to Jesus because they provided *seclusion*. Almost without exception, when Jesus undertook a lengthy prayer session, He *demanded* seclusion and would often go to great lengths to get it. He taught men to enter into the secluded atmosphere of a closet to pray. Obviously the point of the teaching was not to confer a special sanctity to a closet, but closet prayer was contrasted to prayer that was given in prominent places to "be seen of men" (Matthew 6:5).

All this is not to make public prayer illegitimate. Indeed, Christ engaged in prayer in very public places on occasion. Yet the great thrust of His practice and teaching would indicate that we should endeavor to be relieved of as many physical distractions as possible when we pray. However, there will be times when prayer needs to be offered in public places. When these times come, we should at least strive for emotional seclusion. Jesus' cries from the cross were given in a very public location, and yet the very earnestness of the appeals make it evident that He had emotionally entered into the closet. So strive for physical seclusion whenever possible, but always be emotionally secluded in prayer. Never pray to impress men with your piety.

Posture in Prayer. With some dear folk, the physical position of the body is the crucial issue in effective praying. Some will argue strongly for a kneeling position, while others insist that if you really want to have the whammy in your prayers, you had better have your hands lifted up above your head. All of this reminds me of a poem I came across some time ago.

The Prayer of Cyrus Brown

"The proper way for a man to pray,"
Said Deacon Lemuel Keyes,
"And the only proper attitude
Is down upon his knees."

"No, I should say the way to pray,"
Said Reverend Dr. Wise,
"Is standing straight with outstretched arms,
And rapt and upturned eyes."

"Oh, no, no, no," said Elder Slow,
"Such posture is too proud:
A man should pray with eyes fast-closed
And head contritely bowed."

"It seems to me his hands should be
Serenely clasped in front,
With both thumbs pointing to the ground,"
Said Reverend Dr. Blunt.

"Last year I fell in Hidgekin's well
Headfirst," said Cyrus Brown,
"With both my feet a-stickin' up
And head a-pointin' down:

"And I made a prayer right then and there,
The best prayer I ever said,
The prayingest prayer I ever prayed
A-standin' on my head."

SAM WALTER FOSS

From my study of biblical prayer, I would have to concur with
Cyrus Brown. The position of the body is, at best, secondary. The
reason Cyrus Brown prayed most effectively in the well was that he
was in dead earnest! It is heart attitude, not physical position, that
makes prayer effective.

Duration of Prayer. Christ's practice of prayer leaves the question of prayer duration uncertain. It is obvious that on certain occasions Jesus prayed for great lengths of time. Once, at least, He prayed all night. Yet His longest recorded prayer (*see* John 17) can be read in a few minutes. Many of His prayers were in the nature of short, spontaneous outbursts.

Some have inferred from our Lord's rebuke of vain repetitions (*see* Matthew 6:7) and long, pretentious prayers (*see* Mark 12:38–40) that Christ opposed lengthy praying as such. However, as our previous study of these passages indicates, such was not the case in either instance. Yet I believe that the words of D. L. Moody would fit the sentiment of the New Testament. I'm told that Moody once said most men's prayers should be "cut off on both ends and set on fire in the middle."

Pray as long as you have earnest needs to lay before the Father. Pray as long and as often as those needs cause you to feel disposed to do so. It would be out of harmony with Jesus' prayer principles to maintain that an hour spent in prayer is necessarily more effective than five minutes. After all, we are all different, and these differences will no doubt reflect themselves in prayer habits. Some will gravitate to one or two rather lengthy sessions of prayer each day. Others will be prone to have more times of prayer, but of shorter duration. I personally lean in this latter direction, but both are acceptable New Testament practice.

Yet it becomes apparent that prayer is a real barometer of the spiritual attitude of a man. A person sensitive to his own needs and the needs of others will pray often. This certainly was true of Jesus. If you are "tuned in" spiritually, you will be sensitive to needs and driven to prayer with increased frequency and intensity. If this is not true in your life, it probably indicates that spiritual stagnation has set in.

Protocol in Prayer. So far as the actual mechanical procedure of voicing a prayer to God is concerned, neither Jesus' practice nor His teaching gives much by way of emphasis.

Yet many well-meaning folk insist that proper prayer protocol includes the phrase "in Jesus' name" in the format. However, we have seen that such a verbalization was not the basic intent of Jesus' rather lengthy teachings on the subject. The total absence of such a verbal formula in the many prayers recorded in the Book of Acts and the Epistles argues strongly that such was never intended.

Very much along the same line, a prayer need not always conclude with the phrase "if it be Thy will." The overwhelming majority of prayers in the New Testament did not conclude with such words. Again, this is to be essentially an attitude which may or may not be verbally expressed. Even the simple "Amen," though certainly not forbidden, was never actually used by Jesus to conclude any of His prayers. The "Amen" at the conclusion of the Lord's Prayer (*see* Matthew 6:13) is not included in the earliest and best manuscripts of the New Testament and, therefore, was probably not part of the inspired text.

Jesus never taught or practiced any special sanctimonious prayer vocabulary as part of proper protocol. Jesus prayed in the same vocabulary which He used in normal conversation. What I am trying to say is that you need not feel you must pray in King James English! Now there is absolutely nothing wrong with praying in King James English, but don't feel you *have to!* Pray in the kind of English (or whatever language it might be) you feel most comfortable with.

The only issue of protocol given any real attention by Christ was the matter of address. To whom should prayer be offered? In the life and teachings of Jesus, little doubt can be left as to the answer to such a question. Every prayer of Jesus was addressed to the Father, aside from one agonizing outburst from the cross—and even in that single exception, the address was "My God." In light of the fact that His previous outburst was "Father, forgive them . . ." (Luke 23:34), there can be little doubt that in crying, "My God," He had reference to the Father.

Likewise, in His teachings Christ uniformly instructed His followers to address prayer to the Father. Now, I'm not saying that if you inadvertently addressed a prayer to Jesus or the Holy Spirit it would not be heard. Remember that the main thing in biblical prayer is the attitude of the heart. If the heart is right, the prayer is getting through. Yet we should strive to follow the explicit teaching of Jesus and address our requests to the Father.

17
Prayer Conditions and Concluding Remarks

All of us are interested in having our prayers produce effective results. We do not merely want to pray but we want to pray successfully as well. The Bible makes it clear that it is possible to "ask amiss" (James 4:3) and not see effective results from our praying. Therefore, the matter of prayer conditions is of extreme importance.

The Conditions Necessary for Effective Praying

A foremost theme in Jesus' teachings on prayer was the specific conditions necessary to insure successful praying. As already noted, prayer is not essentially constituted as a series of rules and formulas, yet in Jesus' prayer principles there are certain clear-cut conditions taught as being essential to effective prayer. Jesus marks out four factors as primary conditions for successful praying: divine will, faith, abiding, and asking "in my name."

Divine Will

A careful study of the four conditions makes it apparent that they all revolve around the one basic concept of praying in accordance with the divine will. Every prayer must conform to God's will. In Jesus' prayer principles we find the type of teaching which considers the triumph of God's will the triumph of prayer. No warrant is ever given to justify prayer which is consciously in conflict with the divine will. If you should ever approach God and say, "Father, I know this is contrary to Your will for me but I don't care—I demand that You give it to me anyway," God will not be under any obligation to answer that request. Indeed God will, at times, possibly answer such prayers to teach us the consequences of self-will.

Christ often made statements to the effect that His all-consuming passion was to do the Father's will. The classic example of this was His agonizing experience in Gethsemane where He cried, "Nevertheless not my will, but thine, be done" (Luke 22:42). In all the many and varied prayers of Christ there was never the slightest hint of rebellion against the Father's will.

The very concept of prayer as taught by Christ necessitated a primary submission to the Father. Christ did not teach prayer as demanding things from God but as the request a child makes of its parents. A child trusts superior wisdom, reposing in undoubted love and desiring success in no particular petition which may be inconsistent with the superlative will of the Father. Even more explicitly, Jesus taught His followers to request definitely the accomplishment of the Father's will both in heaven and on earth (*see* Luke 11:2).

Faith

At times Christ conditioned successful praying upon faith. Faith in the biblical sense invariably involves a person as its ultimate object. Even in certain instances where faith might seem at first glance to rest upon divine promises, reason dictates that it is impossible to believe in a person's promises without having confidence in the person making the promises. Prayer-faith, then, is a trusting confidence in the Father. It is not simply confidence in the Father's power but also in His total Person. This would involve His love, wisdom, and goodness, as well as His ability.

Prayer-faith is not to be sort of a hit-and-miss affair, but a continuous attitude. It is to be a deep, implicit, trusting confidence in the Father, to the point that even as the request is being voiced, it believes that the request is being heard and seriously considered. It is a confidence that knows that if the particular request is out of harmony with divine will, the infinitely good and wise Father will answer in accord with His perfect will.

This kind of faith carries with it an inescapable expectancy. Often Jesus gave clear-cut indications of expecting the Father to hear and answer even while the request was being made. Once this expectation was evident even before the petition was actually voiced.

Some have found it somewhat paradoxical to pray with real expectancy and, at the same time, pray with genuine submission to God's will. To put it by way of a practical illustration: If I pray for rain, why expect it to rain? If it is not God's will, it won't rain anyway. I fully realize the problem and do not feel I have resolved it as yet to my complete satisfaction. Perhaps our expectancy is not so much that the precise thing asked for will be given in exactly the way we have in mind, but rather that the Father has indeed heard and is acting upon our petition in the best possible manner commensurate with His wisdom and love.

Now if you honestly have no confidence in God, it is absurd to pray. It's like asking a man for something and having absolutely no confidence in him. Such a thing is ridiculous! If you find yourself in such a spiritual condition, concentrate on developing your faith, because successful praying demands faith. A full discussion of how faith grows is beyond the direct range of this book. However, for those who are really interested in pursuing such a study, I recommend my book *Let's Live!* wherein I devote an entire chapter to the subject.

Faith can and should grow, but I want to make it clear that there is no such thing as instant faith. Perhaps the simplest way to understand faith development is to pose the question "How can I gain confidence in another person?" If you think about it, you will discover that you gain confidence in a person by getting to know him. Remember when you first met your closest friend? At first you had little confidence in him; as you got to know him, you gradually gained confidence. As you discovered what a right and reliable person he really was, you gradually learned to trust him completely. God is a person, a very reliable Person. The more you get to know Him, the more confidence you will have in Him.

How does a person really get to know God? One very excellent way is through God's Word, the Bible! As you daily read and meditate on God's Word you will discover what kind of a person God is. As you do this, your faith will grow. That's why Romans 10:17 states, "So then faith cometh by hearing, and hearing by the word of God." Do you want your faith to grow? Hear what God is telling you. You will then pray really believing that God not only hears but also will act upon your requests in accordance with His infinite wisdom. "All things are possible to him that believeth" (Mark 9:23).

Abiding

A third prayer condition definitely stated by Christ was that of abiding. As a prayer condition the concept involves the maintenance of a vital, communal relationship by reliance upon Christ and by being open and receptive to His teachings. The dual ideas of trust and submission seem heavily involved. Thus an abiding Christian would be one who is trusting in Christ, submissive to Christ, and thus living in obedience to His teachings. Obviously such a believer would be in a relationship of the most intimate communion with Christ.

To be successful in prayer, one must first be successful as a Christian. He must be an "on the ball" Christian. Repeatedly in the New Testament there are correlations between practical daily living and successful praying. Peter informs us that a man's prayers can be "hindered" by improper conduct toward his wife (1 Peter 3:7). So praying and practical daily living go hand-in-hand. If you are not living right, you will not be praying right. It's as simple as that! I've known people who grew terribly exasperated with God because He hadn't answered a particular prayer. With a little probing it became very clear, even to them, that they were living carnal, disobedient lives. The problem was not with God or with prayer but with them!

It thus becomes obvious that abiding is directly related to the will of God. It would be impossible to be abiding in Christ and be in rebellion against God's will. Abiding is simply another way of saying, "Thy will be done." Obviously, then, petitions voiced by a believer who is properly abiding are assuredly granted in God's own way and in God's own time.

"In My Name"

Most Bible scholars agree that the pinnacle of Jesus' teachings on prayer was reached when He gave His followers the startling invitation to "ask any thing in my name" (John 14:14). This was a privilege that no disciple had ever exercised up to that point. Christ clearly stated that it was a fantastic opportunity reserved for the new age that would begin with the formation of the body of Christ (the church) at Pentecost.

Asking in His name was directly associated with accomplishment! This would be the way His followers would be able to do the "greater works" after His departure (John 14:12). By asking in His name they would be able to produce permanent fruit. Prayer in His name was set forth as *the* vital function of the believer in order for the work of God to be accomplished upon the earth. It involved a mighty partnership which makes the disciple responsible to ask and the Father responsible to do. Thus both the believer and God are *responsible partners* in an enterprise of accomplishment. God's obligation is just as real as the believer's. If the believer asks in His name, God has obligated Himself to do! In some mysterious manner, God has chosen to condition some of His mighty acts upon human asking! I do not pretend to have the answers to all of the complex theological questions involved. But if a person takes the language of Scripture at face value, there can be no other conclusion.

It is obvious that praying "in my name" does not involve simply attaching the phrase "this we ask in Jesus' name. Amen," as a sort of magical formula to the end of a prayer. It is obviously based upon a new relationship between Christ and the believer. It is organic, vital, and cannot be dissolved. The "in my name" relationship is very close to, if not completely synonymous with, Paul's concept "in Christ." To pray in His name means to ask from the vantage point of the new and privileged position of being *in Christ* as part of His body! However, it is not only to be in Christ but also to consciously realize that you are in Christ and believe you can ask on that basis. As with all spiritual blessings, they are of no value until we realize and actually believe we have them. Every child of God is blessed with "all spiritual blessings . . . in Christ" (Ephesians 1:3). Yet many Christians continue to live impoverished lives because they either don't realize who they are and what they have, or they don't really believe it.

Likewise, every believer is in Christ and is, therefore, qualified to exercise the privilege of asking in His name. Yet only those who pray, consciously aware of their privileged relationship in Christ, are truly praying in His name.

A second factor obviously involved in such praying is that of mediation. To petition from the vantage point of a vital union with Christ implies that our petitions are voiced through the meritorious mediation of Christ. It should be remembered that the effectiveness of Christ's death makes prayer possible. Had there been no Calvary, there could never have been a Pentecost, and hence no "in Christ" relationship or "in my name" praying! It should also be remembered that "in my name" praying is acceptable because of *who He is* and not because of *what we are*. So His death makes this kind of prayer possible, and His life makes it acceptable.

In the third place, petitioning in His name means to ask the Father with the full authority of Jesus Christ. You are in Him and therefore can ask as He would ask! This gives to the believer an inevitable confidence in prayer. A lesser employee in a huge corporation might go to a bank with a draft in the name of the firm with a confidence he would never enjoy should the check be simply in his own name! The name of the corporation gives authority to the draft and confidence to the one presenting it. We do not petition the Father in our name *but in His!* It is as though Christ countersigned our drafts on the bank of heaven. Thus we pray with authority and confidence.

Concluding Remarks on Prayer Conditions

Prayer, when biblically conditioned, will be infallibly answered. This is because the conditions involve a person not only being in a vital spiritual union with Christ but also in intimate, communal fellowship with Him. Anyone meeting the biblical prayer conditions will be voicing that prayer with the provision (expressed or unexpressed) "Not my will, but thine, be done" (Luke 22:42).

The Bible contains quite a few clear-cut instances where sincere, earnest prayers of good people were answered by God with a loving "No!" Moses, the mighty man of God, prayed that he might go over into Canaan, but the request was denied (*see* Deuteronomy 3:23–25). Paul, the great Apostle, prayed for the removal of an affliction, but the affliction was not removed and for very good reasons (*see* 2 Corinthians 12:8, 9). Yet neither of these prayers were unanswered! The request, in each case, was not granted, but the prayers were answered and the answer was no.

When a request is refused, it is as truly answered as when it is granted. Indeed, the accomplishment of God's will is the supreme goal of the person who prays biblically. Such a person will realize, as did Paul, that refusal is evidently the only answer possible in accord with the Father's love and wisdom. A child may cry for a razor, but a loving parent will refuse to give him one. Many a person has lived to thank God for His refusal of their agonized entreaties. I know of one young lady who said that if God had answered every prayer of hers, she would have married the wrong man seven times! A man truly praying in faith will realize that God never refuses without a reason, because prayer-faith is a submissive trust in the total Person of God! A final wrinkle in all of this is that at times God's negative response can be simply a temporary delay rather than a final denial. Moses eventually did enter Canaan, but by a better way and in better company. A seeming refusal may be simply a delay. It always pays to await God's time.

The Value of Prayer

The fact that prayer is capable of producing definite results in both spiritual and material realms is self-evident in Jesus' life and teachings. Almost without exception, the prayers of Jesus produced objective results. By "objective results" I mean that Jesus prayed and a dead man came to life. Jesus prayed, and a disciple's faltering faith did not completely collapse. Jesus' praying affected people and things outside Himself. It cannot be shown by either the practices or precepts of Jesus that prayer was ever simply an exercise in psychotherapy. Christ never looked upon prayer as a means of just talking out His problems and thereby achieving a certain release from anxiety.

Now it cannot be denied that there are many instances where prayer can be seen to have a secondary but real psychological value. Such psychological results are generally seen more or less as side effects in the prayer life of Jesus. At times He would deliberately pray in the presence of His disciples. He would voice requests in their hearing. He would inform them that He had prayed for them. Obviously the intent of these actions was that the knowledge of such things might produce a desired psychological effect upon these men. However, let it be said again that such effects were *never* the primary purpose of prayer.

Indeed, the only possibility of finding any psychological value in prayer is dependent upon the fact that prayer has objective value. Now think about that statement and let it sink in! A man who stops believing that God really hears and answers prayer in an objective manner will very soon lose all psychological value in prayer. In fact, he will most probably quit praying altogether.

Thus biblical prayer is far more than simply achieving a psychological release by verbalizing one's innermost feelings. It is the primary human responsibility in the outworking of God's program on this earth. Time and time again, Jesus assured His followers that the Father would respond to properly conditioned prayer. If you have trouble with divine sovereignty in all of this, I can only say again that God has decreed the means as well as the ends. It would appear that prayer is one of those God-ordained means.

The Goal of Prayer

Prayer in the life and teaching of Jesus was to be for benefits that are primarily spiritual in nature (guidance, cleansing, protection, etc.). Yet prayer, even for these legitimate spiritual benefits, should never be for the selfish purpose of personal development alone. Rather I should pray for these things so that I can be built up in order to more effectively carry on the work of God *so that He will be glorified.* Personal edification is a secondary result, never the primary purpose or ultimate goal of prayer.

It would do us all good to take inventory of our petitions every once in a while. We should ask, "Why do I want God to give me this?" or "Why do I want God to accomplish this in that person's life?" If we are desiring things for our own good reputation or comfort, we are off base. If we are seeking things for our pastor so that his career might be advanced, we are petitioning in a manner that is foreign to the prayer principles of the New Testament. Such praying is very normal and natural to ego-centered humans, but it is simply not biblical.

Personal blessings are a result of the kind of praying which thrusts a person into the main stream of life for the glory of God. But this blessing will never be reached if it becomes the purpose of the prayer rather than the result. The prayer "Bless me" is never valid unless the purpose for offering it is "that I may be a blessing, in order that God may be glorified."

A Parting Prayer Shot

What can I expect to happen if I begin to pray in the fashion advocated by Jesus Christ—I mean really begin to take prayer seriously and begin to labor in it fervently? There need be no doubt at all because Jesus clearly told me what would happen! (*See* Matthew 7:7, 8.)

The first thing I can expect is that God will *always* answer biblical prayer. He won't just answer it some of time, but *all* of the time. In God's own way and in His own time He will, with infallible certainty, respond to biblical praying.

You and I as evangelical believers have absolutely no right to doubt the veracity of prayer! If I were to ask you how you know for sure that you are saved, I trust you would respond by pointing to the categorical promises of God in the Bible, whereby He assures salvation to everyone who personally receives Christ as Lord and Saviour. You would inform me that you know you are saved because you are trusting in the promises of God as recorded in the Bible. Yet that same God in that same Bible also promises "Every one that asketh receiveth" (Matthew 7:8). Now if there is any possibility that God might go back on His promises to answer prayer, how do I know He will not back down on His promise to save me? If I can doubt the veracity of prayer, I can, by the same logic, doubt my very salvation!

No, my friend, God will not back down on any promise. He is a covenant-keeping God who cannot lie. So rest assured, if you really begin to pray, God will answer! He may not answer as quickly as you desire. He may not answer in exactly the way you have in mind. But, bank on it, He *will* answer.

God will not simply answer but also will always answer with good things (*see* Matthew 7:9). He loves me too much to give me just anything. To me this is a tremendous prayer safeguard. I'm quite sure that with my limited mental capacity and from my narrow view of reality, I often ask God for the dumbest things, much as a small child cries out in all sincerity for a peanut butter and jelly sandwich five minutes before dinner. This guarantees that regardless of how stupid my request might be, the Father will always answer with the best.

A friend of mine was flying to Portland, Oregon a few years ago. The pilot announced that the airport was fogged in and the plane might not be able to land. My friend, thinking of all the work he had at his office, began to fervently pray that the plane would land. His wife, viewing the situation from the ground, began to pray, "Lord, don't allow the plane to land." The plane didn't land. Instead, it flew up to Tacoma, Washington and deposited its passengers there. Immediately all of the passengers began findings ways to get down to Portland. A young businessman approached my friend and asked him if he would like to share the expense of a rental car back to Portland. You guessed it. My friend led the businessman to a saving knowledge of Christ. God answered both the prayers of my friend and that of his wife with good things!

Listen! My Bible tells me that battles were won because people prayed. It tells how weather conditions were changed drastically because a man prayed. It informs me that men were released from prison because Christians prayed. The God of the Bible is our God, and He is still in the prayer-answering business. I know that this is true. I've tested the veracity of prayer many times.

Several years ago I became distressed with the editorial tone of our college newspaper. It reflected neither the goals of the college nor the attitude of the average student. My first reaction was to grab the telephone and start political maneuvering, but I thought, "No, God says the way to get things done is through prayer." I found two other professors equally burdened and we began to cry out to God specifically about the paper and its staff. After a year of fervent prayer, without any human solicitation on our part, the paper suddenly fell into the hands of "turned on" students. For two years now we have had a student newspaper that is a plus factor so far as spiritual objectives are concerned and is making a positive contribution. How do I explain it? Prayer!

Quietly, unassumingly, God answers prayer. Often He will do it in such a normal and natural manner that if you are not careful, you will fail to realize that a real miracle has taken place. I once was the pastor of a small church, and each Wednesday evening as the men would gather for prayer, I could always count on those men voicing at least one petition that evening. The great burden of their hearts was for their young people. Week after week they cried out for God to move among the youth of the church. Now frankly, that church had the deadest bunch of teenagers I had ever come across, and I confess that as the men would pray, I had little or no faith that their requests would be answered. After I had been in the church for about eighteen months, I was sitting in my office one afternoon when the thought suddenly hit me, "Hey, we no longer have a bunch of deadbeat teenagers in this church. These kids are really with it now!" The Lord had answered the persistent, fervent prayers of those men, but it had all come about in such a quiet, unassuming manner that I hadn't realized a miracle had actually taken place.

We need to reprogram our thinking. We are all naturally "do" oriented. When a need arises or a problem appears, our natural inclination is to roll up our sleeves and start doing! Yet God says, "You ask and I will do" (*see* John 14:13). A matter needs to be taken care of in the church. What do we do? We call a committee meeting and if we are lucky, we will spend one minute *asking* and fifty-nine minutes *doing*. Then we wonder why nothing happens. I submit to you that it's because we are not operating by God's prescribed formula "If you ask, I will do." What the church of Jesus Christ needs today is not more organizing but more agonizing.

A survey was recently taken among many leading evangelical churches throughout this country and it was found that the one factor they all had in common was a total lack of effective prayer in the life of the church. No wonder so little ground is gained for the glory of God. Clever promotional programs may fill parking lots, but when all the activity is over and the dust settles, so little is really accomplished. Paul urged us to be instant in prayer (*see* Romans 12:12). James told us that the effectual, fervent prayer of a righteous man avails much (*see* James 5:16). He told us that we have not because we ask not (*see* James 4:2). Jesus said, "If you ask, I will do." You would think that we would get the idea.

I realize that when so many pressing needs cry out for attention, it doesn't make sense to sit back and pray. Prayer, from a human vantage point, defies common sense. But do you know something? God has a way of making good sense out of nonsense. God clearly tells us that the conflict we are waging is a spiritual battle and, therefore, our weapons are not to be fleshly and earthly, "but mighty . . . to the pulling down of strong holds" (2 Corinthians 10:4). One of the big guns in God's arsenal is prayer. Believe me, there is no greater work you can do for your pastor, your church, or your missionaries than to labor for them fervently in prayer (*see* Colossians 4:12).

It all really boils down to this: Either prayer works or it doesn't! Either God is telling us the truth or He isn't! My challenge to you is this: Try it out! I mean really try biblical prayer for six months. Relentlessly cry out to God concerning specific matters, in the manner advocated in this book. Keep a written record of these specific requests. I promise you that at the end of six months you will be addicted to prayer in a wholesome sense. Let's begin today to do God's work in God's way!